THE FOUNDATION OF EVERYTHING

THE FOUNDATION OF EVERYTHING

Genesis 1-3

Kevin Horton

ELM HILL

A Division of
HarperCollins Christian Publishing

www.elmhillbooks.com

The Foundation of Everything
Genesis 1-3

Published in Nashville, Tennessee, by Elm Hill, an imprint of Thomas Nelson. Elm Hill and Thomas Nelson are registered trademarks of HarperCollins Christian Publishing, Inc.

Elm Hill titles may be purchased in bulk for educational, business, fund-raising, or sales promotional use. For information, please e-mail SpecialMarkets@ ThomasNelson.com.

Library of Congress Cataloging-in-Publication Data

Library of Congress Control Number: 2018946231

ISBN 978-1-595557865 (Paperback)
ISBN 978-1-595558121 (Hardbound)
ISBN 978-1-595558152 (eBook)

CONTENTS

CONTENTS

INTRODUCTION

The first pages of the Bible cause great turmoil in the minds of many well-educated people because the words of this book are contradicted by much of what we have been taught in twenty-first-century education. Geology teaches us that this world is billions of years old (deep time). Biology makes use of deep time to allow for the evolution of life. Evolution teaches that it is through death and struggle that life continuously improves and advances. In evolution, death is a vital selection mechanism in the removal of less evolved life forms. This death-selection mechanism is imagined as the means in which random changes in DNA is filtered to advance higher life forms.

When one opens the Bible, you are given a totally different scenario. Life was specially created on this earth and not very long ago. The creator of life is not death and struggle as Darwinian evolution teaches. Rather the Creator is an all-powerful intelligent Being. He willfully created the universe, the planet Earth, and all life therein. God imposed death upon all living creatures as a result of the original sin of the first humans and is a curse, not a creator.

People of faith and those struggling to discover faith are challenged by this battle between science and the Bible. Many Christian believers have decided to consider the first pages of the Bible to be a myth and not to be taken literally. Who is to say, per this view, that God did not simply use evolution to bring about life? Yet when we stop and are honest with ourselves, this compromise causes an ever-present doubt about the validity of the Bible. After all, if it is not correct on the first page, dare we trust the rest of it?

There is much more at stake. There exist issues, questions that people want to ask God, which cannot be answered if the first pages are simply myth. In contrast, these questions are answered when the Bible is allowed to *mean what it says*; let me explain this further: when people of the twenty-first century approach the first three chapters of Genesis, they are tempted to explain away the clear meaning of the original Hebrew text in order to make the text fit into our cultural understanding of origins. But when we allow the Bible to speak for itself following standard rules of Hebrew grammar, it is amazing how much it addresses seminal questions of life. It is then that a person will build a solid foundation for a jubilant life of faith. The first pages of the Bible lay the foundation for all that follows. You might well say that the first pages of the Bible inform us of how everything came to be and forms the true *foundation of everything*! If a person can get a solid grasp on these pages and the issues that are solved therein, you will be building a formidable strength into your life. Your life of faith will become immovable because it is built on a true foundation.

This book is designed to face the skeptics of the twenty-first century head-on and answer questions about science and the Bible. Building up from there, we will clarify issues like gender design and differences, the value of human life, and why your life is significant. We will consider the atheist's key question, "Explain to me, Christian, how your good, all-powerful, loving God could create a world like this one—full of pain, suffering, and death?" In doing so, we will follow the Bible text carefully.

Genesis chapter one begins with creation of everything, so part one will face the science questions surrounding origins. Building upon the answers we discover and the freedom to believe that the Bible is true, we will enter part two, the practical portion of this book. Here we will find answers to key questions of life. This second part will cover major topics in Genesis chapters two and three. This work is not intended to be a word-for-word Bible study. Rather it is a theme-by-theme book. It is intended to help people develop solid foundational concepts of living found in these chapters of Genesis. When a person starts to understand and believe the Bible from the very beginning, they will be building their life of faith on a solid foundation resulting in an *immovable* faith. Let the construction begin!

ACKNOWLEDGEMENTS

I would like to thank the people who gave me editorial advice and work on commas and all the things I should have learned in high school English class: thank you, Jenny Harrold, my sister, Missy Murphy, and my final editor, Susan Thomas. This is now much more readable. I am also indebted to my computer spell checker. Science majors are not noted for their spelling bee awards. I would also like to thank Melanie Richard for her overnight work on the human embryo drawings. Special acknowledgement is due to the first class of the *Big Sky Bible Institute* who first put the bug in my ear to write this work.

To my family, thank you for staying with me and loving me through the losses and trials of this life. Tatjana, my best friend, I would never have finished seminary without your love and support. Remember when it was -20^0, the furnace quit, and I was in Chicago? You still sent me back again and again encouraging me to complete my degree. Chris, Andrew, Aaron, Coleman, and Emma, you always brought out the playful side of me and filled my life with joy. Squirky and Cuckoo-bird live on!

PART ONE

The Origin of Everything

Preliminary Foundation:

Where do we start?

How can we begin an investigation into everything?
What are the trusted sources?

Science?
OR
The Bible?

OR
Both?

ARE WE JUST KIDDING
OURSELVES?

In the age of science:

Are we just kidding ourselves when we evoke God as the Creator?

"Kevin, do you still believe in that creation stuff?" inquired a veterinary colleague at a continuing education meeting. She had a point. The clear majority of scientists overwhelmingly espouse evolution as the origin of life. So, are we just kidding ourselves when we invoke God as the Creator? Are we just perpetuating superstitions of ancient man that we are now beyond? Are the people of the Christian faith blinded or ... is it the other way around?

As we consider these questions and in particular the last one, a story from the history of the sciences will help us understand the way humanity perceives reality:

"For God sakes gentlemen ... wash your hands!" [i]

In July 1846, the Hungarian physician Ingaz Semmelweis began investigating, against the goodwill of his superiors, the 13 percent death

rate of women following giving birth at their hospital due to a disease syndrome named puerperal fever. This fatal disease occurred shortly after giving birth to children in their hospital. Did you catch those numbers? Greater than one in ten women would die a few days after giving birth. Dr. Semmelweis noted that in the adjoining midwife wards, the mortality rate was a little over 2 percent. What can be the cause of such an increased death rate when qualified physicians assist the birthing process?

Breakthrough came in 1847 with the death of his friend Jakob Kolletschka, a fellow physician. Dr. Kolletschka was performing an autopsy examination on one of the women who died from the fever when he cut his finger accidentally with the knife that he was using in the procedure. A few days later he died. Upon autopsy, Dr. Semmelweis noted that his colleague died of the same pathology that was observed in women who died from puerperal fever. Dr. Semmelweis postulated that there was some kind of material or particle that was transferred in the blood of the dead person to Dr. Kolletschka. Maybe this same particle was causing the death of the women.

Today, the most horrific part of the story comes as we understand the common practices of the medical practitioners in the days before there was an understanding of bacterial causes of disease. It was common for a practitioner to arrive early in the morning at the medical facility and immediately perform autopsies on the patients who died through the night. Then, without washing their hands, they went on to deliver the babies! Why wash your hands, which are bloody from the autopsy, when you are going to get bloody delivering the baby? Certainly, we know the answer today and are mortified at what was accepted medical practice of that day.

In Dr. Semmelweis' day, the current scientific disease theory that was dominant in the scientific community for nearly 2000 years was that sicknesses were caused by an imbalance of the four basic humors of the body.[ii] This led them to try and balance the humors with such practices as bloodletting[iii]. The practitioners of the day argued that washing their hands between patients would add a burden to their work and accomplish nothing.

As an experiment, Dr. Semmelweis initiated a procedure of washing hands in a solution of chlorinated lime between patients. By this simple procedure, he reduced the death rate from over 13 percent to 2.4 percent! With that great statistical evidence in his hands, it would be expected that his colleagues would immediately rush to find out how Dr. Semmelweis could save so many lives. Amazingly, the opposite occurred. They ostracized Dr. Semmelweis and laughed at his foolish time-consuming practice that was based upon the premise that particles were being passed from the blood of the dead and this caused disease. In due fashion, Dr. Semmelweis was relieved of his duties!

Why could they not see what was blatantly obvious to him?

Eventually Dr. Semmelweis took a position in Hungary at St. Rochus Hospital where he increased intensity of the protocols and included all instrumentation. He thereby reduced the death rate to 0.85 percent.

In 1861, he published a book explaining his findings and sent them to the medical societies and to leading obstetricians in France, Germany, and England. Sadly, a number of unfavorable reviews were written about his findings. Most of the great minds of science were in consensus: Dr. Semmelweis was a radical fool. After many terrible reviews of his detailed work, they still rejected a few simple procedures that would save the lives of tens of thousands of women.

What do we learn about the scientific community when it comes to ideas that are outside the box, ideas that require a departure from the standard way science and medicine understands things? Radical ideas that push the envelope almost always face strong opposition from practitioners of the "standard" way of seeing things. This pushback can be so strong that they will reject ideas that are replete with evidence to authenticate them. Many lives were lost in Dr. Semmelweis' day because of this failure of human beings to simply look at the data and let it speak for itself.

In 1865, Dr. Semmelweis suffered a nervous breakdown and died in a mental asylum. It wasn't until after he died that the scientific community began to wake up to his radical ideas. This wakeup would require a totally different way of perceiving the cause of many diseases. This would bring about a scientific revolution in medicine! In the middle of his great controversy and out of his great frustration with the scientific community, Dr. Semmelweis was quoted as saying, "For God's sake, gentlemen, wash your hands!"

Why could they not see what was blatantly obvious to him?

The Answer

In 1962, Thomas Kuhn wrote his breakthrough book, *The Structure of Scientific Revolutions.*[iv] In this book, Thomas Kuhn investigated the minds of scientists through the eyes of a scientific historian. The question he was researching holds an answer to the strange behavior of the scientists of Dr. Semmelweis' day. Specifically, Thomas Kuhn was seeking to discover the answer to this question: why does science go through scientific revolutions? He was perplexed by the fact that science seems to be held hostage to ideas that lead them up blind alleys. Eventually they would be forced by their own data to abandon this blind alley. Science would then go through a revolution as it tries to find a new skeletal structure[v] upon which they could hang their data. Thomas Kuhn was perplexed that scientists didn't just change the basic premise earlier. You might say that he expected them to modify the skeletons because of the data. All along the way their data was warning them that they were heading up a blind alley, yet they seemed unable to see what was right in front of them. They were interpreting their data with a wrong premise, a wrong paradigm. [vi]

In answering the question about scientific revolutions, he gives us great insight into why the physicians of Dr. Semmelweis' day were unable to see the revolutionary discovery their colleague had developed. It also explains why so many fine scientists are absolutely convinced that evolution is fact and that belief in a Creator is for those of limited education or knowledge.

Now, let's look at what Thomas Kuhn discovered regarding scientists' inability to see data that contradicts their preconceived conclusions:

Thomas Kuhn discovered that scientists, like all human beings, see the world around them through their paradigms. A paradigm is a preconceived set of rules around which the scientist organizes his data. In Dr. Semmelweis' day, all the physicians organized their data and their observations of medicine around the concepts of balancing the four humors. This was their paradigm and it acted as a filter to all the medical data that they discovered. If the data or observations matched their paradigm, such as the practice of bloodletting that would theoretically balance the humors, then the data was accepted as good science and conclusions and applications were drawn. But when the data presented was dramatically outside their scientific worldview, their paradigm, then it was seen to be unscientific and foolish. Their minds rejected the data because it did not match their preconceived set of rules. In this case, everything Dr.

Semmelweis was presenting had no scientific basis as far as they could see. He was simply adding a burden to the daily routine of the physicians. They could not see the benefits because it appeared to them to be based upon "unscientific" premises, so they rejected it outright.

In the research for his book, Thomas Kuhn discovered that the paradigm is extremely powerful over the ability of scientists to integrate new ideas in their scientific field. The paradigm of the scientist and his or her scientific field function as the skeleton to which they attach new data and new ideas. This helps them gain clarity and organization leading to new theories and procedures. The paradigm is also extremely powerful in keeping the scientists from seeing ideas and data that are radically outside the paradigm in which they were trained. Kuhn proved that the paradigm was so powerful that when data presented is outside the paradigm of a scientist, many of them literally cannot see it. The scientist is blind to that data. It is as though the data does not exist, and therefore they will often reject the data as erroneous.

Today, evolution is the paradigm of science. It is the skeletal structure in which all scientific data and observations are hung upon. There is tremendous pressure applied by fellow colleagues in the scientific community for everyone to present their data in a manner that matches the current evolutionary paradigm. If you are courageous enough, like Dr. Semmelweis, to present data and ideas that are outside the current paradigm, you can expect a great amount of negative response by your colleagues.

Today, most scientific periodicals utilize what is called *peer review*. All researchers know that they must publish articles regularly or they will not advance in their field. As research is completed and conclusions are drawn, researchers prepare their data for publication in a scientific periodical. Their conclusions will be scrutinized by their peers. If they attempt to publish research that is radically outside the current paradigm, they risk not being published. In the research field, failure to publish means to perish. All research requires funding, and funding is based upon publishing. Therefore, there is tremendous pressure on the researcher to publish in accordance with the current paradigm."

The late Dr. A. E. Wilder-Smith[vii] is a great example of this. Dr. Wilder-Smith held three earned PhDs from European universities. Very few people ever attain two PhDs let alone three. A man who earns three PhDs in the sciences should be publishing left and right; editors of periodicals should be hounding him for papers. Yet Dr. Wilder-Smith was almost never published. He submitted many papers and, according to his own testimony, they were rejected offhand because he wrote the papers outside the evolutionary paradigm. He let the data present a case for a Creator. In Dr. Wilder-Smith's day, as it is today, scientific papers that contain creationist conclusions are almost universally peer-review rejected as unscientific.

In my own life, I found it very difficult to shed the paradigm of evolution that I had been taught so diligently in my scientific education. It took many years of studying the data all over again. I had to review much of my scientific training and filter out what was evolutionary paradigm and what was raw data and observation. I then had to ask myself what this data does tell me about the world around me if allowed to speak for itself.

Suddenly, the hand of the Creator jumped out from the page! Now I see the world in a totally different way. I cannot miss the hand of the Creator. It seems blatantly obvious. Consider the amazing capability of a pronghorn (antelope) to run 55 miles an hour across the Dakota prairie. Listen in astonishment as the elk bugle each other across mountain canyons of Colorado in the rutting season. Look once more toward the beautiful maple trees of New Hampshire turning color in the fall. Can you not see design written all over this world? Design implies that there exists a Designer.

Many from the evolutionary paradigm have tried to downplay the idea of a Designer and have somehow imagined design designing itself without intelligence; I have come to understand that such thinking is guided by a (blind-alley) evolutionary paradigm. This forces scientists to reinterpret the obvious because everything must fit their evolutionary

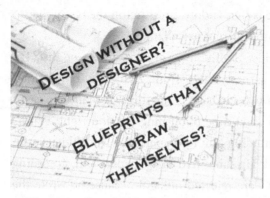

box. So yes, I still believe in "that creation stuff." In fact, I am convinced of it all the more by the new discoveries in science. I have come to conclude that the creation paradigm fits the data; it fits the observations humans make about this world. The creation paradigm matches reality far better than the evolutionary paradigm. *The concept of a Creator as the origin of all that exists is the first and most basic foundation of everything.*

This book is directed to the people of the twenty-first-century. This book encourages people to do one thing: "For God's sake, (ladies and) gentlemen, wash your hands!" Wash your hands of the evolutionary paradigm that you have been so diligently taught!

Returning to an Ancient Paradigm

In the chapters that follow, I want to introduce a new paradigm that is really an ancient paradigm. Some of it will seem downright foolish to anybody who has been well taught. Understand that to the mind of the well-taught, correct paradigms sometimes looks foolish because they are looking at the world through the lens of an errant paradigm. The paradigm (or worldview) of this book is that somebody had to make this world. There is too much design. (More on that is coming.) Design demands a Designer. The worldview of this book further assumes that the Designer of this universe took the initiative to tell us about Himself and how He created this world. He chose to use words as a means of presenting His thoughts to His creatures, namely, human beings. Those words are recorded in the Bible. *The words in the Bible, then, are the actual thoughts of the Creator of the Universe in written form.* This is the worldview that I would like you to consider. I understand that if you have been well taught in the evolutionary worldview, then much of what I say will be radical and may even, at times, seem downright foolish. This is the risk I take when I write outside of the accepted paradigm.

Join me as we examine the first chapters of the book of Genesis in the Bible. In these chapters, the creation of this world is described. The origin of life, the value of humanity, an understanding of why there is pain and suffering, and many other fundamental concepts that explain the world around us will be brought to light. A great many radical paradigm-challenging applications to life will be discovered.

Remember: my purpose is not to write a verse-by-verse commentary. Rather, I will be examining the major life-challenging teachings of this amazing book with a view to reset your worldview to be parallel with the Creator of the Universe. When you set your life in parallel with the paradigm that comes from the Creator, your life will be set upon a solid rock foundation. You will find stability in a solid and trustworthy faith, and that faith will carry you through the worst storms. You will become Immovable. There's one thing I have found to be certain about this life: storms will come. The only question that remains is whether your life will stand the beating. If you build your life upon the solid rock foundation of an accurate paradigm derived from the Bible, then you will one day look back and be amazed at how well you weathered the storms.

Application to real life:

Q: If the evidence for a Creator is so obvious, how come many brilliant scientists are firm evolutionists?

A: To advance in today's scientific community requires extensive training in the current paradigm. Evolution is the paradigm of science today and all who are to advance in science are extensively taught to think and see the evidence they discover through evolution. Like the medical practitioners of Dr. Semmelweis' day, they are blinded by their paradigm.

A: The issue of evolution also is a spiritual issue. The philosophy of atheism finds roots within an evolutionary philosophy. Some people like to "free themselves" from the restrictions that God has on their lives. An evolutionary philosophy does allow people to pursue any lifestyle they choose without restriction.

FOUNDATION TWO

Developing a Trustworthy Source

TWO

SCIENCE AND THE BIBLE:
DO THEY WORK TOGETHER OR
IN OPPOSITION?

In 2005, Dr. Mary Schweitzer reported in *Science* what could be described as the scientific discovery of the century.[viii] When interviewed by *60 Minutes*, she described her internal reaction to her amazing discovery, "I didn't want to tell any-

one." The interviewer fed her a possible moti-vation for this unusual reaction, "You would be ridiculed, right?" She responded, "Yes."

A scientific break-through that you do not want to report ... what is that all about?

Dr. Schweitzer was associated with a project to unearth T-Rex fossil bones from the oldest known rock layer bearing these giants. This was a 68-million-year-old formation. The femur bone of this giant was too large for the helicopter to lift and had to be sliced in half for removal from its remote Montana location. Dr. Schweitzer was sent fragments from the split femur bone. Upon arrival at her North Carolina laboratory, she instructed her technician to use a mild acid to soften the fossilized bone from a small fragment of the specimen. What was left behind was actual dinosaur soft tissue. She had actual T-Rex tissue! This is the real-life stuff that movies like *Jurassic Park* are made from. Her discovery is absolutely impossible since all soft tissue encased in fossilized bone will have been decayed within 100,000 years of burial. Certainly, by 1 million years, not even a trace of soft tissue could be left.[ix] This places a huge burden of proof on the dates given to rock layers. This is terribly troubling to those holding the evolutionary paradigm[x].

As the discovery went forward, she identified dinosaur proteins and what appeared to be blood vessels with nucleated red blood cells in them. On MSNBC she is quoted as saying this about her discovery, "It's utterly shocking, actually, because it flies in the face of everything we understand about how tissues and cells degrade." She went on to say, "A lot of our science doesn't allow for this ... it just doesn't seem possible ... I can't explain it, to be honest." She has since found dinosaur soft tissue in other bones ... even older than the T-Rex.

The problem with her discovery is that it is absolutely impossible for soft tissue to remain intact for much over 100,000 years let alone a million years. Her first reported sample is dated **68 million years old**. The implication of her findings is that this bone is much younger than estimated (like 67,996,000 years younger!).

What is the elephant-in-the-room implication of this finding?

The greatest implication of Dr. Schweitzer's discovery is that all chapters in school textbooks that deal with the age of the Earth, conclusions in many research papers, and the great evolutionary displays in museums like the ones below are in terrible error:

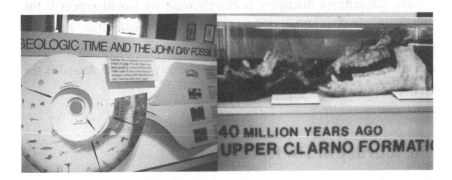

On these displays, the imagined evolutionary development of life over millions of years is graphically presented with great confidence. After all, it has the backing of the consensus of the clear majority of scientists. [xi]

The photo above declares the age of the jawbones discovered on site as 40,000,000 years ago. This is presented clearly and authoritatively. Who but a fool would question it?

Right next to the above displays, this book was presented:

Dr. Schweitzer's discovery flies in the face of the confident displays in countless museums, school textbooks, and research laboratories across the world. Her discovery calls into question the "deep time" that the theory of evolution requires. In reality, the finding of soft tissue of such high quality in a fossil would require the fossil to be relatively young with a date of about 4,000 years. This is because everything we know about tissue deterioration tells us that soon after death the proteins and chemicals of the animal breakdown. Even encased tissue will naturally breakdown. [xii]

Dr. Schweitzer's discovery is exactly what we would expect if the Bible is correct. The Bible, taken as actual history, implies that this world is quite young (about 6,500 years old). Most science and newspaper articles are written in direct contradiction to the way the Bible describes the origins of life. What are we to make of this?[xiii]

The Journey of Dr. Kevin Horton

Let me take you back to my journey as I begin to unravel this issue of science and the Bible:

I guess I always suspected that there was a God.... In time, however science became my religion. I graduated from high school at age seventeen and stepped right into college. I was fascinated by biology and it became my major. My professors at the small college I attended explained to us how life on this planet evolved by chance. As impressionable students, our brains soaked up their words. We understood the ramifications of evolution, though it was never discussed. Oh, yes, if you are religious, you could easily say that God was the one who was behind it all. Biology just explains how He did it. He created life through evolution. Now with that said: do not be mistaken on this; evolution also opens the door to the atheist's view which states that it is just as likely that this world simply evolved *by itself* and that the very idea of God is simply a creation of mankind.

> We all knew that since evolution was true, the existence of God was an open question, an option.

In those days, I had no idea what the Bible said about how God created, so it was comforting to know that I could allow for

God in a scientific world…. But then again we all knew that since evolution was true, the existence of God was an open question, an option.

Evidence of Evolution in Action

In my early undergraduate days, I was taught a simple phrase in my biology courses. This phrase is: *Ontogeny Recapitulates Phylogeny.* The idea behind this phrase, set forth by Earnest Haeckel, was the evidence that convinced me of the validity of evolution. It is quite compelling. It cements belief in evolution to near certainty. Charles Darwin thought this evidence was so compelling that he devoted an entire chapter to it in his later work, *Descent of Man.*[xiv] And since this phrase was so true to my understanding, God, if He exists, must fit into evolution. On the other hand, if He doesn't fit, then His existence most likely is not true.

So what does this phrase, *Ontogeny Recapitulates Phylogeny*, mean? Let me explain it as I was taught in my undergraduate studies. The idea considers human child development in the uterus of our mothers in the very early stages. The growing human embryo, per this theory, passes through various stages. In each of these various stages of development, our growing human embryo "revisits" our evolutionary past. Thus, when a microscope slide is made of an early human embryo, we discover a sort of visual history of our evolutionary past. Look at this drawing:[xv]

The growing human embryo, of which each one of us was at one time, has evidence of evolution in it. In the early stages of development, we discover gill slits. These are evidence

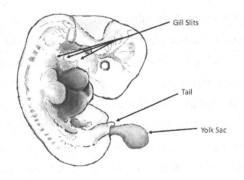

of our evolutionary fish past. Similarly, we find the human embryo to have a yolk sac which is evidence of our evolution from birds. Finally, we discover the growing child has a tail, which is pictorial evidence of our mammalian or monkey evolutionary past. This evidence is nearly conclusive of the validity of evolution. Since this clearly proves evolution, who but a few ignorant fools would question the truth of our evolutionary origins?

Now with this evidence before us, there is a bit of personal history that I need to share before proceeding. During my junior year in college, something profound happened to me that would change everything. I came to believe that Jesus was the Son of God and He died for my sins. I became a Christian. This was a radical leap of faith for a person like me. It was one that would shape my life from that day forward. Through this new faith my fragile marriage, which was rapidly moving toward divorce, began to show signs of life. However, there was a serious problem brewing. It would come to a climax in my first year in veterinary school at Iowa State, and it had to do with *Ontogeny Recapitulates Phylogeny*.

> If the Bible was wrong on such a major point as the origin of life, then the God of the Universe could not have overseen its writing.

Vet school began and soon I found myself engulfed in anatomy and physiology. I was also required to take a course on veterinary embryology that I did not want to take. You see, I had come to really enjoy the new Christian life I was experiencing but this class had the potential to derail Christianity from my life. Here is how: I knew that those gill slits proved Darwinian evolution and I had come to understand that the Bible taught something quite different. If the Bible was wrong on such a major point as the origin of life, then the God of the Universe could not have overseen its writing. In embryology at Iowa State University, a showdown was awaiting me!

I was incredibly busy in vet school. I studied late into the nights and weekends. Embryology class was progressing and I was fearfully awaiting those evolutionary gill slits to show themselves. But the class ended and the gill slits never appeared in any of the books or microscope slides! I was confused. Where were those gill slits?

As it happened (I would now say it was the providence of God), a Creation-Evolution debate was scheduled on Iowa State campus that spring. I took time out of my hectic schedule to witness it. To my astonishment, the creationist put a drawing of a human embryo, like the one I previously showed you, up on the screen pointing out the gill slits and yolk sac. I was on the edge of my seat. My ears were tuned with great intensity to every word he spoke. He referred to the gill slits, the yolk sac, and the tail of the human embryo. *Exactly right*, I was thinking. But where were they in my embryology class?

He then put a slide like this one up on the screen:

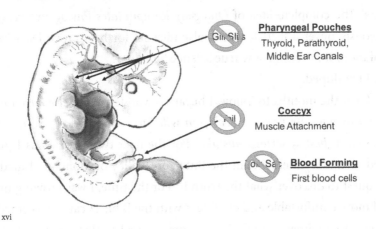

xvi

"The gill slits never existed," he explained to the crowd. My mind raced! What was he saying? He continued to explain that the yolk sac (which is a misnomer of a name) has nothing to do with yolk. It is simply a sack where the early bone marrow cells develop. *Okay*, I thought, *I do remember that from embryology class.* The speaker continued, expanding the discussion to that of the alleged gill slits. Gills are used by the fish to transfer carbon dioxide into the water and remove oxygen from the water. On the growing human embryo, we do see what appear to be little slits. He then labeled these as pharyngeal pouches. *Of course, that is exactly what we called those little slits in embryology class*, I reminded myself. Okay, this was connecting. My mind flashed back to embryology class and the slides we studied. Those exact pouches were labeled in the diagrams in our books. We spent hours examining slides of the developing dog. They had the same pouches as humans. I had learned that the pharyngeal pouches are simply layers of outer skin tissue that fold inward to form the thyroid gland, the parathyroid glands, and the middle ear canals.[xvii]

The speaker continued to explain that the tail of the human embryo is not a tail at all. The vertebrae grow ahead of the legs to facilitate proper muscle attachment. As the embryo develops, the legs will of eventually slide down into their proper position removing any semblance of a tail.

The whole concept had been proven to be false for over seventy-five years! The complete idea of *Ontogeny Recapitulates Phylogeny* was outrageously never a fact! It was a false idea set forth to prove Darwinian evolution. It never had any true science behind it.

I felt duped.

Over the months to follow, I began to wonder, *What else have I been taught as absolute proof of evolution will turn out to be, at the worst, a hoax or, at best, a serious mistake?* For the next twenty years as I practiced veterinary medicine in the Bitterroot Valley of Montana, I made it my quest to discover what the truth is. For the time, I was growing more and more comfortable and confident with the Bible because it seemed to project a true image of life. I have come to realize that much of today's *apparent* contradiction between science and the Bible will be swept under the rug without admission or apology as it turns out to be in error. It will be replaced quietly with the newest and latest. That, in turn, will soon be replaced with something else that is new and astonishing, flashing boldly across the headlines. The admissions of error, the findings of falsehood never seem to filter down to the textbooks or the headlines so that our next generation of brilliant minds never hear what they have been taught was wrong. All the while the Bible remains quietly, persistently present-ing its message. No changes will be necessary.

Understand this point:

Science and scientists have great skill and abilities in making obser-vations about the world that surrounds us. The fruit of the work of generations of skilled scientists have produced a lifestyle that is common to this generation of people that was never dreamed of possible a hundred years ago. This occurred because the scientific method works with data that is dis-covered in the present and brings about great inventions that improve our lives.

Science is not, by design, able to authoritatively address the origins and history of this planet and how it came to be filled with life.

When we look to the past and try to piece together how life came into existence, the sci-entific method no longer functions with any degree of certainty. We cannot do an experi-ment in the present time that will fully inform us how life started. Therefore, when a scientist or a textbook begins speaking authoritatively on the subject of origin, we need to understand that they have stepped out of the realm of science. The textbook, the sci-entist, the instructor who ventures into the realm of the origins of life and speaks authoritatively is not representing what science can authoritatively address. Science is not, by design, able to *authoritatively* address the ori-gins and history of this planet and how it came to be filled with life.

In contrast: the Bible is reliable when dealing with this history because it was inspired by Someone Who was there. We have eyewitness reports.

Earnest Haeckel's gill slit postulate has been proven false by modern embryology[xviii]. In 2005, Dr. Schweitzer reported her discovery of soft tis-sue from dinosaur bones. Common sense tells us that fossilized bones millions of years old cannot have blood vessels and soft tissue intact today. Science is not designed to uncover the history of the universe. It can give us clues to the past but cannot *authoritatively* address the past.

Therefore: we would be unwise to use the scientific views of today as evidence against the Bible. The Bible will not change tomorrow since it is a book that includes history. The views of science are in a constant state of change as it addresses new data in the present. Science is about discovery in the present time.

This leaves us with the eyewitness historical reports found in the bible. Are these biblical reports reliable as sources of history of the Earth and the universe we live in? In the chapters to follow, I will let them speak for themselves.

Application to real life:

Q: If the soft tissue from dinosaurs is strong evidence that the T-rex died just 4,000–5,000 years ago, how do scientists age the rocks? Don't they use radiometric dating?

A: Most all the rock layers around the world have all been assigned dates based upon evolutionary time scales, especially in areas where modern geologists have done a lot of work. They are dated first and foremost by the fossils that are found in those layers. In other words, *the fossils date the rocks.* The rocks do not date the fossils. Radiometric dating is then used to confirm those dates. That leaves us to question the basic ideas behind radiometric dating.

Q: How then, do we know how old the fossils are?

A: Many textbooks and museums assign an evolutionary date to the fossils by speculation of how long it would take that animal to evolve. The rocks, then, are dated first and foremost by the speculated time for Darwinian evolution to take place. This is circular reasoning and is the basis of all those dates you find on fossils you buy in rock shops or are displayed in museums. We have no certain method of dating rocks that bear fossils (sedimentary rocks). The only way we can put an accurate age on any rock would be if someone was there when it was made and told us its age.

POINT:

Every week you will see headlines boasting the latest scientific discovery that "proves" Darwinian evolution, the age of the universe, or something related to history of biology. Most of these will be "swept under the carpet" in twenty years as the new data arrives. Remember this: *science is not designed to authoritatively address the history of this world.*

FOUNDATION THREE

How did everything get here?

Everything...
Matter, located in *Space*, and functioning in *Time*...
Where did it all come from?

Have matter and space always been in existence?
OR
Did everything (matter and space) make itself?
OR
Has there been some creation event?

THREE

WHO MADE US? ETERNAL MATTER OR ETERNAL GOD?

You have two choices:
Eternal God or Eternal Matter

M y Uncle Lloyd was a mathematician for NASA in the early days of America's rocket program. He was also an avowed atheist. In one discussion with him, I presented this question, "Uncle Lloyd, what is the origin of matter[1]?" This brilliant mathematician paused and then admitted, "For that, I have no answer."

How did the universe begin? This seminal question is one that baffles the most brilliant of people. Many of us have no real answer to this question. However, this very question of the origin of the universe, of the origin of our world, is a difficult question to avoid as one gazes into the heavens on a clear starry summer night.

Many people today view the universe as the creator itself. The vast universe with its immense loci of power is imagined to be capable, by nature of itself, to create life simply by chance happenings in time. With that in mind, some even consider human life as an intrusion. Consider the words of the late Stephen Jay Gould to which the picture below sets the appropriate feel:

xix

The human species has inhabited this planet for only 250,000 years or so—roughly .0015 percent of the history of life, the last inch of the cosmic mile. The world fared perfectly well without us for all but the last moment of earthly time—and this fact makes our

---

[1] Matter is defined as all the physical substances that make up the universe. Our bodies are composed of matter. All chemicals are matter

appearance look more like an accidental afterthought than the culmination of a prefigured plan.

Moreover, and more important, the pathways that have led to our evolution are quirky, improbable, and unrepeatable and utterly unpredictable. Human evolution is not random; it makes sense and can be explained after the fact. But wind back life's tape to the dawn of time and let it plan again—and you will never get humans a second time.

We are here because one odd group of fishes had a peculiar fin anatomy that could transform into legs for terrestrial creatures; because comets struck the Earth and wiped out the dinosaurs, thereby giving mammals a chance not otherwise available (so thank your lucky stars in a literal sense); because the Earth never froze entirely during an ice age; because a small and tenuous species arising in Africa a quarter of a million years ago has managed, so far, to survive by hook and crook. We may yearn for a "higher" answer—but none exists.

This explanation, though superficially troubling, if not terrifying, is ultimately liberation and exhilarating. We cannot read the meaning of life passively in the facts of nature. We must construct these answers ourselves, from our own wisdom and ethical sense. There is no other way.

– Stephen Jay Gould[xx]
Paleontologist, essayist, and humanist

Is that how we got here?
Could this be the explanation to the origin of all that exists?
Was it just a grand accident?
How did the stars, those giant energy factories in space, get started?
Did they just start themselves?

There are two major ways to view this world and the life upon it:

- This world is eternal and somehow self-originating to its present form
- It has been created by someone, some power, outside of it.

Dr. Gould (quoted above) gives us a good feel for the former view in which the world, by quirky accident, created itself and all the complex life forms on this planet. Maybe you noticed that in this view, Dr. Gould sees mankind as an intrusion. He further makes it clear that should we try this experiment again, it would never happen the same way. We are just a roll of the dice. And yet in this essay he states that it is not random.... Most importantly he interjects his motivation, his philosophy: "We may yearn for a 'higher' answer—but none exists." We are here for a time and then gone.

Nothing really matters.

Nothing has any purpose.

According to Dr. Gould, if you live for a week or 100 years, in the end it really does not matter. Life is nothing but a cosmic accident only to disappear to dust. Somehow, he takes that emptiness and turns it to liberation and exhilaration. I can only guess that he feels free from any restraint from God. His actions no longer matter so he is free to live his life as he pleases. There is no ultimate accountability. Right and wrong are a matter of opinion. Morality is simply what you want it to be. Consequently, when you die everything is over. There is no accountability to any higher power. This is what is liberating about this humanistic view of life: it frees mankind from any accountability. If God does not exist, then no one exists to whom you must give an account when life ends. You are free to do as you please. If you get away with something, fine. If someone is harmed but you gain, fine. There exists no God to answer to later.

That is fine ... if it were true.

It is not.

It is not true.

The proof is in the candle:[xxi]

Consider a candle purchased from the store. Its long slender shaft comes to a fine taper with a clean white wick protruding from the end. This candle has energy stored within it. When you light the candle, the chemical energy stored in the paraffin begins to be released in the form of heat and light. The candle shortens as the energy is released. The paraffin will eventually be burned up and all its energy will be released.

Our candle, shown above, is brand-new from the store. It is in perfect condition. One hundred percent of its energy remains within it. All it requires is for someone to bring a flame near so it may begin releasing its energy.

In contrast, consider another candle. It is shorter and it is burning as we speak.

<u>What can we say about this shorter burning candle?</u>

- We can say that this candle no longer contains the full amount of energy it originally had.
- We can also state quite certainly that before it was lit, it contained 100 percent of its energy.
- We *cannot* say exactly how much of the original energy is gone (for we do not know for sure how long it originally was).

Since it was lit sometime in the past, a portion of its energy has been released in the form of light and heat that has filled the room. Similarly, a portion of its energy is still in the form of potential energy stored up in the wax. This potential energy is represented by the remaining height of the candle. The potential energy will be released into the room if the candle is allowed to burn all the way to the table upon which it is sitting. At that point (unless the table starts on fire!), the candle will go out.

Now think of the universe with all the galaxies full of stars as multiple candles. One day, sometime after our birth, we stare up at the sky and are amazed by the sight of all those twinkling lights, all those *twinkling candles* above us. We recognize that the candles, the stars, are burning. Therefore, we can conclude a couple of things:

1. There must have been a time in the past when these stars were unlit and ready to begin releasing their energy. They were like that unburned candle above: 100 percent of their energy was contained within them.
2. There also must have come a time (in the past) when these candles (stars) were lit. At that moment, they began to burn and give off light and heat to the universe. From that day onward, they contained somewhere less than 100 percent of their original energy. A portion of their original potential energy has been released to the universe.
3. We *do not* know how long they have been burning for we do not know their original size.
4. We *do* know that there will come a day when they will burn out.

What we are beginning to define is called thermodynamics, the study of change in energy.

There are certain laws that govern how energy changes in the universe. Let us consider the *First Law of Thermodynamics*:

Think of the universe as that one giant candle. Let's place that candle in a giant mirrored-glass bubble that is perfectly insulated. This glass bubble does not let light or heat escape. The total amount of energy found inside that bubble is the same if the candle is unburned, half burned, or totally consumed. The energy total is the same. The only thing that changes is the form of the energy.

Here's what I mean by that:

- The bubble may be dark and cold with the unlit candle.
- It will be warmer and brighter once the candle begins burning.
- Finally, it will be hot and dark when the candle is burned out.

In the first case, the sum total of the energy that was inside the bubble was in the form of the unlit candle; the energy was not released yet … but it was there. In the second case, the energy was partly released and partly in the paraffin. In the final case, the energy was completely released to the space of the bubble and now nothing is left to burn. In all three cases, the total amount of energy in the bubble is the same. The only thing that changed was the *form of the energy.*

1. With the unburned candle, the energy is all potential. None of it has been released to the bubble.
2. In the second case, some of the energy is still potential in the unburned portion of the candle. Some of the energy has also been released in the form of light and heat.
3. In the last case, all of the energy has been released to the inside of the bubble. It is still the same amount of energy as the unburned candle.

The only change in the energy within this bubble is **the form** the energy is in. As the candle burns and eventually burns out, the energy moves:

$$\text{Potential energy} \rightarrow \text{Kinetic energy} \rightarrow \text{waste heat.}$$

(Paraffin)   (Heat and Light)   (Heat)

We have essentially defined the First Law of Thermodynamics. This first law states that the sum total of the energy of the universe does not change. The only thing that does change is the form.

<u>Now let's apply this to our universe:</u>

There was a day sometime in the past when our sun was unlit and contained 100 percent of its potential energy. This was when it was in its perfect condition. It was like a brand-new tapered candle just purchased from the store. Sometime after that, the sun was lit. It began burning and releasing energy to the universe. There will also come a day when the sun has released 100 percent of its energy. The sun will burn out just like a candle on the table.

Now think of the sum total of all of the energy the sun will release over the ages of its existence. All of that energy was in the form of potential energy on the day before the sun was lit. On the day it runs out of energy, 100 percent of that energy has been released to the universe in the form of heat, radiation, and light. Now consider the universe on both days. On the day before the sun was lit, 100 percent of the sun's energy was within the universe. It was in the form of potential energy. On the day when the sun burned out, 100 percent of the sun's energy is still within the universe, only this time all the energy has been converted to heat. There is no change in the *quantity* of energy in the universe. The only change is the form.

The First Law of thermodynamics is called the Law of Conservation of Energy. Energy is neither created nor destroyed; rather it is changed in form. There is no creation of energy nor is there destruction of energy in the processes of the burning of the stars. As a star burns, it releases energy in the form of heat, light, and radiation. There is **no creation of energy**. Nothing within the normal processes of the burning of the stars creates energy. The burning of stars **is not a creative event**. It is simply **a conversion event**. The implication of this law is that the universe cannot create itself since nothing is being made.

Remember this: *The implication of the First Law of Thermodynamics is that the universe cannot create itself.*

Okay, if there is no creation of energy going on in the stars, what is going on?

This brings us to the Second Law of Thermodynamics. This law looks at how far the candle has burned. This law also considers the fact that an unburned candle has 100 percent of its energy available to do work. (In the view of physics and chemistry, *work* is performed using energy. Think of energy and its usefulness in *work* like gasoline in the tank of your car.

Once you drive the car and use the gasoline, it is no longer available for driving. That is what scientists mean when they speak of energy being available or unavailable for work.)

Let's return to the candle. Once you light that candle some of that energy has now been lost to heat (it is still energy and still in the bubble but it is not available for work anymore). The longer the candle burns the greater the amount of the original potential energy will have been dissipated into the sphere and is unavailable for work. *The amount of energy no longer available for work is called **entropy**.* The Second Law of Thermodynamics states that energy goes from a state of usable energy to a state of <u>un</u>usable energy. The longer the candle burns the shorter it gets. The length of the candle that has been converted into heat represents entropy. Entropy is energy that is no longer available for work. Look at the three candles below:

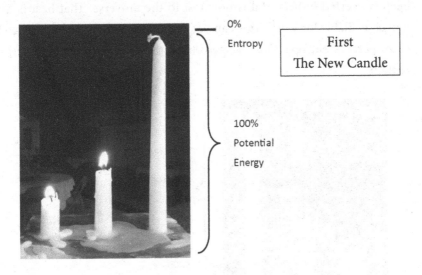

0%

Entropy

First

The New Candle

100%

Potential

Energy

Consider the tallest candle, the one above. This candle has never been lit. Therefore, 100 percent of its potential energy remains in the form of the paraffin. Its entropy is zero.

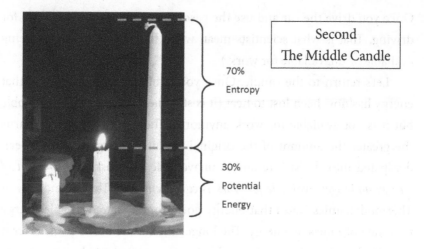

Now look at the middle candle. It has been burning for quite a while: 70 percent of the candle is gone. That means 70 percent of the energy has been converted to heat and is now lost to the universe. That heat is no longer available for work. This candle's original energy has been reduced to 70 percent entropy. Only 30 percent of the original potential energy remains.

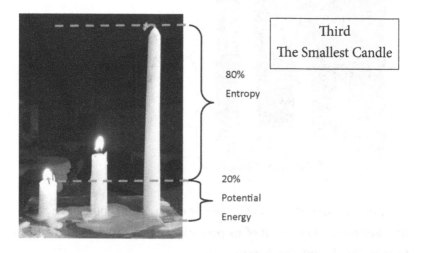

The last candle, the one on the left, has been burning the longest: 80 percent of its original energy has now been changed to entropy and is no longer available for work. Only 20 percent of its original energy remains as potential energy. Because the candle is burning, a portion of that potential energy is being converted at this very moment into kinetic energy. Kinetic energy is useful for work immediately. In this case, 80 percent of the candle has been converted from useful energy into entropy. Basically, the second law of thermodynamics defines what we all know … that is: things burn up.

Now consider this: you have traveled to a little secluded cabin that your family owns high up in the mountains. You unlock the door and swing it open to discover a lit candle burning on the kitchen table. This is one of the brand-new candles that you brought up to your cabin last fall before you closed it up for the winter. Immediately, information has flashed through your brain. You begin looking around the room to see who it was that lit the candle. You know instinctively that this candle could not be still burning from when you locked the building up six months earlier.

The point of this illustration is quite simple: burning candles can also serve as a form of a clock. You knew that this candle had to have been started sometime in the recent past. That is why you experienced the cold shiver up your back. You were fearful of who was in your cabin. The reason you are fearful is that you know enough about candles to know that they will not burn all winter. Candles cannot burn for an eternity. There has to be a time in the recent past when the candle was started.

Apply this to the universe about us. We come on the scenes of this world and one day we look up at the stars and realize that they are burning candles. This tells us information immediately. We realize they are not eternal candles. They must've had a start. Every candle you see burning had to be started. When you see a star burning in the heavens you know that it must have been started. *At some point in time past, every star in this universe had to be lit.* Every star had to have a beginning. Stars are not eternal. *The implication of the second law of thermodynamics is that the universe full of burning stars had to have a beginning.*

Let's put this together. What are the implications of these laws?

1. First law of thermodynamics:
   a. the stars in the heavens cannot start themselves
2. Second law of thermodynamics:
   a. the stars had to have a beginning[xxii]

We have a universe full of stars that had to have a beginning and they cannot start themselves. What is missing? Someone or something outside of the universe had to start it. Dr. Gould believes in a self-generating universe. Yet the laws of the universe tell us something different. They shout of a universe that is limited and had a beginning.

You have two choices:

- You can place your faith in eternal matter that self-created
- You can place your faith in an Eternal God
  o Who is outside of time, space, and matter.
  o Who created time, space, and matter.

Only the latter is consistent with the observations of the universal laws.

Let's add one more ingredient into our discussion: when it comes to the origins of the universe, no human being was there. Therefore, this issue must be approached with an element of faith. We can place our faith in the creative abilities of eternal matter, or we can place our faith in the creative abilities of an eternal God. But the laws that govern heat make it clear that this universe had to have a beginning, and it could not create itself. Something, someone must have started it.

The reason my brilliant atheist uncle Lloyd had no answer for the self-origin of the universe is that there are none. The universe cannot create itself and yet it must have had a beginning.

Which will you believe in? Eternal matter or Eternal God?

It is this very question that separates Judeo-Christianity from all the other religions and philosophies of the world. The very first verse of the Bible addresses this issue:

Genesis 1:1 (NIV84)
¹   In the beginning God created the heavens and the earth.

This text is a translation of the original Hebrew. There is something extremely important hidden from English readers in this text. It would have been obvious to the readers of Hebrew.

In Hebrew, generally speaking, the word order is:

Verb → Subject → Object.

This contrasts with English where the noun (subject) is usually the first word of the sentence. When the word order is changed in Hebrew, there is an intended emphasis. This also happens in English when the verb is placed in front of the noun. Consider this little statement: Yoda said, "Turning, the trees are." Notice that the verb comes before the subject in this sentence (this would be the normal order in Hebrew but abnormal for English). By changing these words around, the emphasis of the sentence has been dramatically changed. The emphasis is not on the trees but on the process of turning. In the first sentence of the Bible, there is a compound word that we translate into the phrase "in the beginning." This word is out of order for Hebrew and so it is emphasized. Theologians call this switching of the word order *"fronting."* When a word is fronted, emphasis is being placed upon it. If this sentence was in normal Hebrew word order, it would begin with the word "created." But in this particular case, the compound word referencing time ("in the beginning") is placed before the verb. That peculiar word order would have caused the Hebrew reader to realize that this text is emphasizing the idea of "beginnings." It could be said that it is written in ***bold italics***.

The first word of the Bible is fronted and it deals with time. This ancient book written by men who were supposedly barely out of the Stone Age began their book with *the origin of time*. How is that possible? Maybe someone inspired them, someone Who was there!

There is more: when time began, it began with the creation of "the heavens and the earth." In the Bible, we can find three different usages of the word "heavens." This Hebrew word can speak of the atmosphere above the earth. This would be the realm of birds (Genesis 1:9). The second usage speaks of outer space (Genesis 1:14, Ex 32:13), the realm of stars. The final usage of heaven is the awesome throne room of God. Often this is referenced to as the "highest heavens" as is in 1 Kings 8:27 (also see Gen 28:17).[xxiii] The definition most appropriate in this verse is the second case, that is, the realm of the stars or outer space. A contemporary translation would go like this: "In the beginning, God created outer space."|

Also created with the heavens is "the earth." In the Bible, this word refers to the earth or land or even minerals and dust. "The earth," then, includes the Hebrew idea of physical matter. Simply put, it is all of the "stuff" of the universe: paper, ink, air, bodies, and chemicals to name a few.

Let me expand our contemporary translation: "In the beginning, God created outer space and filled it with matter." When this simple first verse of the Bible is carefully considered, *we discover that the Bible <u>begins</u> with a concise statement that declares the origin of time, space, and matter*!

What is most astonishing about this above statement is that it wasn't until the time of Einstein that people have come to understand that time and matter are intricately related. Time is simply a measurement of the intervals that it takes for events to occur within matter. *Time really has no meaning without matter.* Because the human race is produced from matter, human minds, therefore, function by chemical reactions. All of these reactions take time. <u>Time is meaningless without matter.</u>

Not only does the Bible give us an origin of time, space, and matter but it informs us of the originator of these elements. You might say the Bible tells us Who made the candles and lit them. The Bible says God created all of these. The Bible speaks of an intelligent All-Powerful-Being who is outside of time and space. He is the **uncaused cause** of all that exists. The laws of thermodynamics clearly tell us that this universe had to have a beginning; they also inform us that this universe could not create itself. Therefore, there must be something, someone outside of the universe who started it all.

This astonishing book, the book of Genesis in the Bible, is an ancient document that was written some 3400 years ago, long before the age of scientific discovery. And yet we find that its first words are very advanced scientifically. Most religions and philosophies of the world either begin with an eternal universe, or they don't address origins at all. Contrastingly, this ancient document, the Bible, begins by telling us the origins of time, space, and matter. It also tells us that God created it all.

The origin of time, space, and matter is distinctive of Judeo Christianity which are the only original religions in the world that have a definitive origin of all that exists. Islam, borrowing from Judaism considerably later (the ninth century AD), speaks of an origin similar to Judeo Christianity because *it borrowed the concepts* from them. Christianity includes the concepts from Judaism because we use the very same Scriptures, the (Jewish) Old Testament. The New Testament is a fulfillment of the promises found in the Old Testament.

Modern science, however, struggles to give a scenario on how the universe began. Many years ago I heard Isaac Asimov speak of these matters. He was discussing the Big Bang as the originator of the universe. Isaac described discussions among scientists as they considered all the matter of the universe. They observed that the matter of the universe is expanding as space expands. When they extrapolate back in time, they conclude that all the matter of the universe was, at one time, condensed into a small ball. Some believed that matter, in this condensed form, was contained in a ball about the size of our earth. Others believed that all the matter of the universe was concentrated in a ball about the size of a golf ball. Either way we are left wondering how this universe came to be like it is, full of stars that are burning in an expanding space.

Mr. Asimov postulated that an instability occurred. Some even believe that this instability required a momentary suspension of the laws of the universe, though it was only a minute fraction of a second. In recent days physicists have been searching for what they called the "God particle." This particle, in their minds and by their equations, would allow the universe to overcome the laws and have the force to create itself into what we now know as our present universe. *Somehow* these forces would allow the Big Bang to occur without outside help.

> Judaism and Christianity are the only original religions in the world that have a definitive origin of time, space, and matter.

Following this Big Bang, matter began to expand rapidly into space (or, more correctly, space expanded into hyperspace). Quantum physics offers the speculation that time had a beginning, but there was never a first moment in time. That seems a little wild to me. I have concluded that some of the research into the Big Bang and the physics thereof are simply a search by mankind to find a way around the obvious implications of the laws of thermodynamics. Interestingly, all of what I have said above relative to these laws has not escaped the minds of the theorists. In order to remain free from the concept of God and to remain totally naturalistic in their scientific presuppositions, it is necessary to develop theories for the uncaused cause (other than God). To be truly naturalistic, the Big Bang must begin without any help. It must occur without anyone causing it.

However you look at it, many scientists currently believe that it was this Big Bang that gave rise to the universe as we know it. Notice that a colossal element of faith is required for this Big Bang to occur. Remember, in a natural universe without God, the Big Bang must start itself. There can be no outside help ... no outside being, intelligence, or power to start the universe. Why would this instability occur? How did this expanding universe organize itself into the fantastic world of stars, planets, and galaxies that we observe today and all without any outside help?

Christianity states quite clearly and quite simply that there was somebody Who started all of this, namely God. God spoke and all of time, space, matter, and energy came into existence. This is an exceedingly superior statement to place one's faith in. *Please note that either way, each individual must apply faith when considering the matters of origins.* You can place your faith in the idea that God started the universe, or place your faith in the idea that matter started itself.

So, what can we conclude about these issues? Could this massive universe create itself? The laws of science say no.

The bottom line is this: *whatever you decide*, it will be a matter of faith. You can have faith that matter created itself or you can have faith that someone created it. *When it comes to concepts-of-origins, all people must apply faith.*

It all comes down to this:

- You can believe in eternal matter
        Or
- You can believe in eternal God.

The decision is yours. The Bible poetically gives this charge to all people:

Psalm 19:1–4a (NIV84)

1   The heavens declare the glory of God;
     the skies proclaim the work of his hands.
2   Day after day they pour forth speech;
     night after night they display knowledge.
3   There is no speech or language
     where their voice is not heard.
4   Their voice goes out into all the earth,
     their words to the ends of the world.

The Psalmist is making it clear that an intelligent man or woman who looks out at the stars at night must conclude someone made this universe.

It doesn't matter what language is spoken or how much education you might have received. The heavens make it clear: *Someone made this universe*. That someone is named God.

Application to real life:

It really matters which view you take. If you place your faith in eternal matter as the creating force that made you, then you are free to do whatever you like because in the end we all just die and return to matter.

On the other hand, if you believe that there exists a Creator, then what you do in this life does matter. When your life ends, there is Someone to Whom you owe an answer to how you lived your life.

The problem with the former view is that it is contrary to what we observe in this universe and its laws. So the universe itself shouts out, "Someone Made Me!"

Which will you place your faith in:

- Eternal matter - you have to convince yourself to believe this one
- Eternal God - you actually do know this one is real ... you may not like it ... but you know it....
  - How do you know it?
    - The stars are shouting this truth every night.

Application to real life:

POINT: The first verse of the Bible has an origin of time, space, and matter. No other writings in all antiquity compares to this simple verse in its deep grasp of basic scientific reality of the universe.

FOUNDATION FOUR

Is there really a God?

God...
Does He really exist?

Is God just the opiate of the masses?
OR
Is there really a God?

FOUR

PROVE TO ME THAT
THERE IS A GOD

Each of us is on a life journey. When we as youth become cognitively aware, questions of origins begin to develop in our young minds. What follows is a little window into my early days as I sought to know what reality is.

I turned the key on and started my old white Chevy. I was sixteen to seventeen years old. The radio crackled out these words from the deteriorating grid covering the speaker under the dash, "Last week I proved to you the existence of God; this week I will continue from there...."

It was Sunday afternoon and our local rock and roll station's regular programing gave way on Sundays to satisfy the needs of the religious folks in town. I would normally just switch it off, but those words caught my attention. I wanted to hear what that raspy preacher had to say. I shifted the three speed on-the-column to neutral and leaned forward straining to hear. If someone could prove to me

> If someone could prove to me that God exists ... that would be worth hearing ... because that changes everything!

that God exists… that would be worth hearing… because that changes everything!

I listened for 5–10 disappointing minutes. Evidently, this preacher considered his last week's work on this topic concluded. He was now focused on the application of last week. Rats! I really needed to hear the previous week's message. I wanted someone to prove to me that there really is a God! If someone could do that, it would be life-changing.

> ➢ Does God exist?
> ➢ And is the Bible His record, His communication to humanity?
> ➢ But what if the Bible does not fit reality?

Here is the bottom line:

Can a rational, educated person be a man or woman of faith, specifically faith in the message of the Bible, without compromising his or her intelligence? Do you have to *"check your brains at the door"* as Josh McDowell[xxiv] coined it?

When the first page of the Bible is approached, the dilemma is just that: you must *check-your-brains-at-the-door* **or** you must rethink everything you have been taught about this universe. However, there is a third approach that many people try: they simply reinterpret the first chapter of the Bible so that it *appears* to be in harmony with naturalistic interpretations of the scientific data.

The challenge of Genesis Chapter 1 is this: this chapter is written in a simple chronological format. If the first chapter of the Bible is read at face value, the implications are that this earth is quite young, somewhere less than 10,000 years old. Many creationists and biblical theologians would place that figure around 6,500–7,000 years old.

Have we not been taught that the universe is billions of years old? Most museums and national parks have items on display that are labeled millions of years old.

So what are we to do?

- Do we check our brains at the door and just believe the Bible blindly and say this so?
- Do we change the way we interpret the Bible so that it matches Darwinian theories and timelines?
- Do we question the underlying theories that are espoused by many scientists and scientific institutions and somehow twist these theories to match the Bible?

When Christians approach this first chapter of the Bible, they apply various methods of interpretation. Some take a **literal approach**, interpreting this first chapter as historical narrative, a story from history. They note that the text quite plainly speaks of six literal days of creation that progress one after another. They note that each day ends with this statement, "and there was evening and there was morning the first (or second...) day." The literalists would argue that if you wanted to tell people that this universe was created in six literal days, you could not be more specific than to speak of the evening/ morning cycle of the Earth's 24-hour day. If you take this radical approach to the Bible, you will come to these conclusions:

> When the first page of the Bible is approached, the dilemma is this: You must check your brains at the door
>
> **or**
>
> You must rethink everything you have been taught about the universe.

- The Earth is only about 6,500–7,000 years old
- It only took six literal days to create this Earth.

- Nearly all the fossils found all over the earth are from the flood of Noah.
- All the living creatures of earth were created fully formed and perfect.

It is important to note that the literal approach only places short time on the earth. Time in stellar space is not defined in the bible. This is interesting because in the last century we have come to discover that time does not flow at uniform rates throughout the universe. Gravity concentrations in an expanding universe makes time unpredictable and quite likely vastly variable throughout space.

The greatest drawback to this view is that it is in direct conflict with the age of the earth taught by the vast majority of public and private universities, museums, and schools.

Another group of people will approach this first chapter with *some version* of a **theistic evolutionary** interpretation. By theistic evolution, I mean that God used evolution to create life on this earth. For this approach to work, there must be adequate time for evolution to occur. Therefore, many theistic evolutionists believe that when the Bible speaks of God creating on day one or day two, the word "day" is referring to a period of time, not a single 24-hour day. In this view, a day may represent millions of years of time. People of this approach will quickly refer us to 2 Peter 3:8 which says, "But do not forget this one thing, dear friends: with the Lord a day is like 1000 years, and 1000 years like a day." This is a convenient approach to Genesis because it allows us not to *check-our-brains-at-the-door* while maintaining some credibility with modern consensus views on origins and the age of the earth. This later view on time is often called the **Day-Age theory.** The day-age theory is not confined to theistic evolutionists: it is also used by people who subscribe to special creation by God. They simply view the timeframe in Genesis to be nonliteral.

The greatest theological weakness of using the quote from 2 Peter is that it is applied inappropriately to Genesis. The text does make a case that God views time differently from us. He is outside of time. Now...what does that mean? What does it mean to be outside of time? I cannot personally grasp the full implications of being outside of time. I imagine it this way: God can look at you reading this book right now *and* at the same moment—at the same 'time'—view you millions of years in the future. That means that everything He promises about the future will happen. He is looking at future events as happening right now. He is also looking at you reading this book right now. The problem of applying this to Genesis is this: just because God is outside of time does not mean that when He speaks about periods of time to us humans who are inside of time He is not precise. We will see later that the Genesis text is very precise on the meaning of "day" being 24 hours.

An older approach is called the **Gap Theory**. Adherents of this approach believe that two different worlds have been created. The first world was created in Genesis 1:1. The second world was recreated in Genesis 1:2. Here's what the Bible says in those verses:

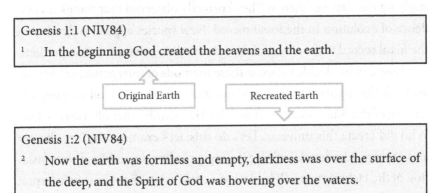

> Genesis 1:1 (NIV84)
> ¹ In the beginning God created the heavens and the earth.

Original Earth   Recreated Earth

> Genesis 1:2 (NIV84)
> ² Now the earth was formless and empty, darkness was over the surface of the deep, and the Spirit of God was hovering over the waters.

The gap theory states that God created the heavens and the Earth and then Satan rebelled against God. God destroyed that Earth and recreated it in Genesis 1:2. In the mind of many gap theorists, the fossil record that we find all around the world is a remnant of this first world that God subsequently destroyed. They (the fossils of the dead animals and plants) represent a history of the world that was created first. The animals living *these days* are from the recreated world of Genesis 1:2.

The advantage of this method is that it accounts for the fossil record (i.e. that we find fossils animals and plants in rock layers indicating that these lived at an unknown time in the past) and still allows a more literal approach to what follows. They would view the six days of creation that follow Genesis 1:1 as literal 24-hour days. However, the straightforward weakness of this theory is that the biblical evidence of such a creation and recreation is very strained. It seems to be inserting an entirely different world and a vast amount of history between two verses without cause.

A highly prominent view among evangelical churches is what is called **progressive creationism**. In this view, God creates different life-forms gradually over extended ages on the earth. It is important to point out that according to this view, God created these various species or kinds and they are not the result of Darwinian evolution. In this view, evolution is not the creator; God is the Creator. Progressive creationism differs from the literal view into that it accepts millions of years of Earth history by applying the day-age theory. They correctly observed that there's no evidence of evolution in the fossil record. New species appear to develop in the fossil record without any of the intermediates that evolution predicts.

How can we decide between these methods of interpretation? Setting aside all the arguments, a simple question remains: if God oversaw the writing of the Bible, which method did He intend? After all, He's the One Who did create this universe. Let's do this: let's examine the first chapter and observe it in detail. Let's see if simply reading a good English translation of the Hebrew text will lead us to a conclusion about how to interpret this controversial chapter of the Bible. Please understand that the original writing of Genesis, given to us by inspiration of God, was in the language of Hebrew. Ultimately, some reference to the Hebrew manuscripts will be needed and quite helpful.

Let's begin with the <u>First Day</u>:

Genesis 1:1–5 (NIV84)

[1] **In the beginning** God created the heavens and the earth. [2] **Now the earth** was formless and empty, darkness was over the surface of the deep, and the Spirit of God was hovering over the waters.

[3] And God said, "Let there be light," and there was light. [4] God saw that the light was good, and he separated the light from the darkness. [5] God called the light "day," and the darkness he called "night." And there was evening, and there was morning—the first day.

<u>Hebrew techniques helping readers keep track of topics:</u>

In English we use tools like italics, underlining, and bold text to emphasize and organize written materials for increased understanding. In Hebrew narrative, it has been observed that putting the noun in front of the verb, which is out of the normal Hebrew order of the verb – noun – object, is a technique for helping the readers understand the organization and emphasis of the text. It has already been noted that in the very first verse "beginning" was fronted (it is out of order). The author was emphasizing the origin of time. The second verse also contains fronting. The Earth is fronted. The author intends us to see that verse # 1 takes up the topic of the *origin of time*, which is linked to the origin of space and matter, while verse # 2 focuses on *the earth* and its physical development.

<u>The Earth:</u>

The text is now focusing on the creation of the earth; the author wants us to see that the earth was formless and empty in form. It seems to imply that the matter was quite chaotic/disorganized. The spirit of God began to hover or vibrate over the surface of the earth. The implication is that this vibration is bringing the mass together and organizing it. We can speculate that it is being formed into a sphere. Also notice that it is dark, which will be rectified shortly.

The next thing to observe is that various creative acts of God will come about by the command of God. Verse three begins with the words "and God said." We can observe a pattern: God speaks, and creation events follow.

Now look at verse four: Light, as a form of energy, is created and is shining on this new earth. Then God *separates* light from darkness. What can this mean? Day and night are being established on Earth. This seems to be an account of the beginning of the rotation of the Earth. I would speculate when the Spirit of God was hovering (or vibrating as the Hebrew word implies) over the waters, He set the mass of the Earth in motion. The Spirit of God set the Earth rotating at a specific speed.

With the Earth now rotating, there exists a precise means of quantifying time. The major means of measuring time by humanity is the rotation of the Earth and the day / night cycle. We eventually divided the time of one rotation into 24 hours of 60 minutes of 60 seconds, allowing more precise coordination of time among people. If I am correct and the rotation of the Earth began in verse four, it is possible to conclude that the 24-hour period begins in verse four. This verse makes a case for a literal 24-hour period of time for each of the "days of Genesis chapter 1." Once again remember the Bible really does not address time off the surface of the Earth. But in Genesis it does address time on Earth by defining the day with the parameters: "evening and morning." This phrase along with the "separating light from darkness" makes a strong case for taking the days of creation as literal 24-hour long days. Evening and morning can only occur on the Earth as a result of rotation of the planet.

Day Two:

> Genesis 1:6–8 (NIV84)
>
> 6   And God said, "Let there be an expanse between the waters to separate water from water." 7 So God made the expanse and separated the water under the expanse from the water above it. And it was so. 8 God called the expanse "sky." And there was evening, and there was morning—the second day.

Outer Space

What is the expanse here? This is one of those issues that are not easily understood. Henry Morris, who might well be named the father of the modern creation movement, spoke of this expanse as the atmosphere...the abode of the birds[xxv]. Another view presents the idea that God began to expand outer space at this juncture. This view fits better with the details of days 4, when the stars are formed in the expanse and day 5 when the birds fly on the face or surface of the expanse. In this latter view, the atmosphere is located on the intersection of the earth and the expanse (outer space). Further, God *names* the expanse. The NIV poorly translated the Hebrew word [shaw-my-eem] as "Sky." This is the same word used in verse 1...and interpreted as "Heavens." Therefore, the evidence leads me to interpret the "expanse" as describing outer space, the abode of the stars.

Expanding Space

The Hebrew word for "expanse" speaks of an extended surface or something that is spread out.[xxvi] This interpretation neatly presents the idea of outer space as it is being expanded, stretched out. (See Job 9:8, Ps 104:2, Isa 40:22,44:24, 45:12, 51:13, Jer 10:12, 51:15, Zech 12:1) This becomes important when we consider starlight and time.

Day Three

> Genesis 1:9–10 (NIV84)
> 9 And God said, "Let the water under the sky be gathered to one place, and let dry ground appear." And it was so. 10 God called the dry ground "land," and the gathered waters he called "seas." And God saw that it was good.

Notice again that God speaks and things happen. This is followed by the divine pronouncement that everything is good. Also distinguish that in verse nine, the text mentions water "under the heavens (same Hebrew word as in vs 8)." This is making certain we are understanding that the waters spoken of here are surface waters. In verse 10 we see that dry land appears by the gathering of the waters and seas. The description is of the seas being gathered. God spoke to the seas and "desired that they be gathered" so that dry land will appear. It does not seem to speak of the land rising so much as the water being pulled away. One possibility of what is being described here is the development of the deep-sea trenches into which the water would drain, allowing dry land to appear.

> Genesis 1:11 (NIV84)
> 11 Then God said, "Let the land produce vegetation: seed-bearing plants and trees on the land that bear fruit with seed in it, according to their various kinds." And it was so.

The next thing to be created by God is vegetation. Vegetation is the critical link between the energy of the sun and the energy needed by all animal life. Plants will take the energy from the sun and convert it into chemically stored energy such as sugars. Vegetation must be created first so that animal life will have a chemical energy source.

The Genuine "Origin of the Species"

It is critical that you observe that vegetation was created according to kinds. What does the Bible mean when it says animals and plants are created by kinds? We could name this section as the Bible's version of *The Origin of the Species*. Long before Darwin and his famous book, this famous book, the Bible, already contained *The Genuine Origin of the Species*.

In the last 150 years, science has uncovered the mystery of the "specie." We now understand what makes one seed develop into a tree and another into a weed or a bush. The miracle power of the different species is found in the DNA molecule in the center of the cells of each individual plant or animal. The DNA molecule contains information or code that is put into action by the various organelles within the cell. [An organelle is a microscopic structure within cells that function like chemical factories, energy-producing power plants, or even garbage disposal systems. More on this shortly.] The code is rigidly followed by the cells of the plant, thereby causing it to develop very specifically into the type of plant that it is coded for. The code for an apple tree is significantly different from that for an orange tree. *The code is the key.* The code contains the information that makes the apple seeds grow apple trees. All apple seeds contain the code that will specifically make them grow into another apple tree. The code of an orange seed is the specific code that will make it grow into an orange tree and not an apple tree.

The question that must be dealt with here is: *where did the code come from?*

The Bible informs us that there exists a superintelligent Spirit Whom we call God. God has the intelligence to develop the code for the DNA that is specific for apples. He also developed all of the chemical structures (organelles) within the cell that are necessary to read that code and put it into action so that the cells of the seed will divide and grow into an apple tree.

The concept of "kind" informs us that God developed the code with a significant but **_limited_ diversity** in it. This diversity would allow the particular plant "kind" to survive in various environmental conditions and stresses. Each "kind" had sufficient code variations that would allow for slightly different offspring. This variation would help the "kind" to thrive in varying environments.

Let me give an example:

Consider an apple tree that is very short. It might survive in areas where there is less rainfall. A taller tree might have a better survival rate in a place where deer and other animals would like to browse on its leaves. The taller tree would grow its leaves above the reach of these animals. This taller tree would also require more water. A single apple tree will produce many seeds found in its many apples. Each seed has slightly different random combinations of the original DNA code (for apple trees) depending upon the source of the pollen for that particular seed. [Note: pollen blows in and is transported by bees to apple flowers mixing the slight variation of genetics from nearby apple trees. The pollen is the male contribution to the seed.] The slightly different combinations will then give us individual trees that have different survival strengths. One individual seed may produce a tall tree. This tree will have better survival capability if the seed germinates near a water source. At the water source, it will be able to grow tall above the jaws of the wildlife that will want to browse on its leaves. Another individual seed from the same tree may be a short version. If these two seeds happen to land close to each other, the taller version will have the genetic superiority to survive in that environment.

In contrast: take the same two seeds and plant them in another environment where the water isn't as abundant. In this environment the pressure from the wildlife will likely be less, and the smaller tree will have a better chance to survive.

This is simply the theory of natural selection applied to the Biblical idea of "kind." The only deviation from the evolutionary version of natural selection is that the biblical view states that all the information necessary to make the different strengths found in different individuals of a species was *already in the genetic code* of the original created "kind." So, within the biblical concept of "kind," in my view, is the concept that the original "kind" had a diverse genetic code so that the "kind" could survive in various environments.

At this juncture, let me introduce two terms that must be carefully differentiated and will help us understand the different perspectives (the biblical versus natural science perspectives) relative to the origin of the different species we observe in this world. The first term is called micro-evolution and I will associate it with the biblical version of *The Origin of the Species*. The second term is *macro-evolution* and I will associate it with Darwin.

In microevolution (the Bible's version), we begin with a general "kind" of animal or plant that contains sufficient information in its DNA to allow for great diversity of individuals. The biblical "kind" is a word that is broader than the term "species." These original plants contained the DNA information to allow individual plants to have diverse characteristics. These diverse characteristics would allow the plant "kind" to survive varying environmental conditions. This definition of "kind" would be like the taxonomic classification of "family."

Where did the code come from?

Example: The Dog Kind

Let me explain this with the dog "kind" since these animals have a long history of close association with humans. In the original dog "kind," each individual animal contains the DNA information so that larger dogs and smaller dogs can come from a single kind. This would allow the diversification of the "kind" into various species of dogs such as the Australian dingo, the North American coyote, the European Wolf, and our domestic dog species. Time and different environmental pressures compounded by isolation of packs from other packs led to the selection of characteristic we classify as a specific species (like the coyote.)

From a genetic perspective, the coyote contains less genetic information than the original dog "kind" which had the information in its DNA to make all the different dog species that we see today. Here is how that occurs:

Environmental conditions place survival pressures upon individual dogs. In certain environments, dogs with particular traits will flourish whereas other individuals will have difficulty. Each individual's ability to survive, thrive, or perish in a particular environment is dependent on their body characteristics that were dictated by their genetic code. Those that do not survive long enough to reproduce will have failed to pass on their genetic characteristics to the next generation. The genetic code for their body characteristics will have been lost from the local gene pool. If this happens with all of the animals in that locality of a particular body characteristic (such as long hair vs. short hair), then that gene data is totally lost for the dogs in that environment.

The coyote, as an example, has lost the information necessary to make all the other dog types. The coyote species has been isolated long enough that it has lost this genetic information for diversification. This happens as individuals who were unfit for survival within that environment died out without reproduction. With their death, the genetic information is lost from the local "coyote" gene pool. As this loss continues, the animals in that isolated environment become a true species. [Remember: I have defined the scientific classification of "family" as a reasonably close class to what the Bible defines as "kind."] As more specialization occurs by environmental pressure, the ability to reproduce with others of the dog kind will become limited.

What we are describing here is a form of evolution that results in a *loss* in genetic code. If they are breed back to some of the original dog "kind" they may have diversified sufficiently to not be able to produce fertile offspring. If that happens (as it did with donkeys and horses) then there is no going back. Look carefully at the chart below noting that each species originated from the early biblical "kind."

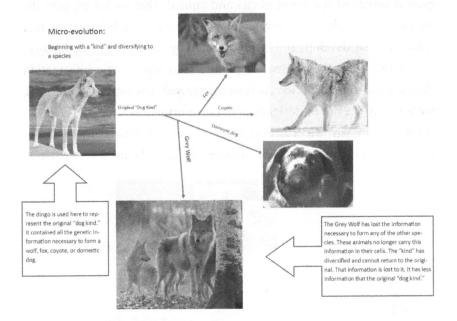

Micro-evolution:

Beginning with a "kind" and diversifying to a species

Original "Dog Kind"   Fox   Coyote

Grey Wolf   Domestic dog

The dingo is used here to represent the original "dog kind." It contained all the genetic information necessary to form a wolf, fox, coyote, or domestic dog.

The Grey Wolf has lost the information necessary to form any of the other species. These animals no longer carry this information in their cells. The "kind" has diversified and cannot return to the original. That information is lost to it. It has less information that the original "dog kind."

What we are describing here is called microevolution. Notice carefully that in microevolution there is a *loss* of genetic code. Some of the information that was in the original DNA molecule of the dog "kind" is no longer available within that species. The lost information is carried on in some of the other species of dogs such as wolves or domestic dogs, but is no longer available within the coyote species. *In microevolution, there is a loss of the information necessary for diversification into other species.* This happens naturally as groups live in isolation from each other in environments that favor certain traits. [To be clear: an environment such as a dry hot desert would favor short hair and smaller bodies. A northern tundra environment would favor longer hair and larger bodies.]

On the other hand, macroevolution, as Darwinian evolution asserts, works in just the opposite manner. Darwinian evolution envisions a world in which DNA information is developing itself through mutations or other means. In macroevolution, plant and animal species begin with very little information and over time information develops itself within individuals to the extent that new species are developed. In this view, the great diversity of species of plants and animals that we see all over the world is the result of the development of new genetic information that spontaneously develops and is **not directed by any outside intelligence**.

In this view, the original dog "kind" has less genetic information than the individual species. As time progressed new information forms, without any Creator or designer, and this information is capable of development of massive structural changes in the individuals. These design changes lead to diverse species. Consider the chart below:

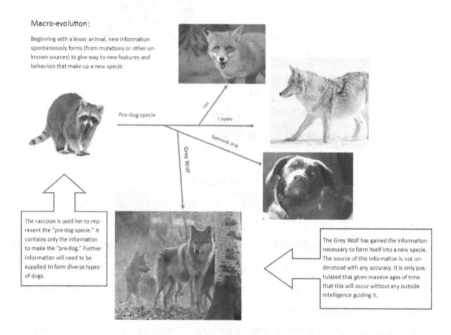

Macro-evolution:

Beginning with a lesser animal, new information spontaneously forms (from mutations or other unknown sources) to give way to new features and behaviors that make up a new specie.

Pre-dog specie

Fox

Coyote

Domestic dog

Grey Wolf

The raccoon is used her to represent the "pre-dog specie." It contains only the information to make the "pre-dog." Further information will need to be supplied to form diverse types of dogs.

The Grey Wolf has gained the information necessary to form itself into a new specie. The source of this information is not understood with any accuracy. It is only postulated that given massive ages of time that this will occur without any outside intelligence guiding it.

How is this possible that new improved code spontaneously arises?

It is postulated that mutations (mutations are mistakes in copying or damage by harmful environmental forces that insert errant code into the DNA) built up sufficiently to develop slightly different animals. Over vast ages of time, these mistakes built up a new version of the code that 'create' changes in animals that give them survival advantages.

On the surface this sounds possible. Here is the serious error: macroevolution fails to recognize that the genetic code cannot tolerate these changes. Mistakes in the code lead to wrongly formed proteins or improper execution of controls necessary for life. Geneticists inform us that over 999 out of 1000 mutations are slightly harmful.[xxvii] It is a very rare mutation that results in improvements of any sort. These improvements also come with a cost to the living creature. With changes in the code there is some loss of function elsewhere in the lifeform.

Let me illustrate the problem with this imagined source of information that self-originates: think of this manuscript. As I typed these words on the page, I misspelled quite a few. Thankfully, we have spell checkers. (Incidentally, the cell has a spelling checker as well. This spelling checker looks for errors and corrects them. But it is imperfect, so some get by. Those that get by are mutations.) If words were left in my book misspelled, it would leave you guessing on what I was meaning. As misspellings increase, the information becomes increasingly unintelligible. Darwinian evolution imagines a day when sufficient misspellings occur that it accidently creates a new sentence. This new sentence will produce a new attribute that allows the animal to thrive in an environment that previously it could not. This new sentence (which has to be in a language we can read) is quite a jump of chance ... yet we can imagine that it could occur with sufficient time. The great fallacy is this: while you could imagine that over millions of years of mutations a new sentence could be developed in one location on the DNA molecule, simultaneously there would also be thousands of *paragraphs* of vitally needed code elsewhere in the DNA loaded down with damaging errors. Did you catch that? We could imagine that over millions of years of mutations that it is conceivable that a new sentence could arise that is readable in our language. But we cannot dismiss the fact that at the same time thousands upon thousands of errors elsewhere in the code would destroy the meaning of the entire book! Sanford named this problem with mutations destroying information as *Genetic Entropy.*[xxviii] Genetic entropy is the gradual destruction of the original genetic code over time by the force of mutations. Dr. Sanford's point is this: the genetic code is deteriorating. It is not improving as macroevolution imagines.

Make sure you understand this conceptual difference between the biblical view of creation of kinds and the Darwinian view of the spontaneous development of species:

1. In the biblical view, an intelligent source (God) created the plant and animal "kinds" with enough diversity in their genetic code to survive in varying environments. As the animals spread out across the earth and faced varying environmental pressures, individuals with characteristics that aided them to survive in a particular environment became predominant. Those individuals made up the reproducing gene pool in this environment. This gene pool, being isolated from the others of their original kind, lost the genetics for diversification. In other environments, the original kind is pressured by different environmental pressures leading to survival of those individuals best suited in that environment. With sufficient isolation, these characteristics, now found in these microenvironments, became so dominant that a new sub-kind developed. These sub-kinds (which science defines as genus or species) have less genetic diversity than the original kind. In the biblical view, the source of the intelligent code is an intelligent being (God). The code was created in a perfect state and over time is subject to deterioration.

2. In the Darwinian evolutionary view, natural processes are imagined that provide the code. We start out with an inferior code that *developed itself* by random processes. [This is a monstrous leap of faith. *There exists no known mechanism in the entire universe that has been shown to develop intelligent code spontaneously within chemical molecules. This is the most unscientific concept in the Darwinian evolutionary view.*] This

code expands and improves by mutations over the course of millions of years. Evolutionists imagine that these mutations will eventually add to the code the necessary information to design new structures. This new information will be sorted out by natural selection over the course of millions of years and eventually lead to successful new structures and new designs that increase a group of individuals' survival capability.

Let's put this code development in perspective

Example:

Consider the box of disks to the right. Let's put the name *Microsoft Windows on* the box. If you try to purchase these, you may have to pay nearly $119.99 (as of winter 2018). I can buy these disks (below and to the right) for about $.35 each:

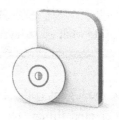

What am I spending the extra $119.64 for?

Sure, we all know the answer: it is information. It is code. The Windows disk contains a massive code that has been intelligently designed using the accumulation of information developed in the minds of literally tens of thousands of peo-

ple over the course of the last century. This information has cumulated into the design of Windows Operating Systems. We are purchasing intelligent information. The disk is not what you're purchasing. That's only worth $.35. You are purchasing the information, the code, which has been burned onto the desk. Windows 10 upgrade contains about 3.5 gigabytes of intelligent information to update a computer. The human DNA molecule contains the most compact information known. Your DNA contains 1.5 gigabytes of information that is specific to build you.

Consider carefully what Darwinian evolution is asking you to believe.

The evolutionary view on the origin of life is that a very specific code that contains the information to produce proteins, regulate actions, and much more that we are just discovering spontaneously developed in a primordial muck billions of years ago ... all by itself. In this view, we are asked to rely completely upon the natural properties of matter to develop intelligent code without any intelligence.

> The natural properties of matter are destructive not constructive.
>
> Evolution wants us to imagine a world that is contrary to what we see every day.

Is this reasonable? Do we actually observe this happening? I do not know of a single instance in which the natural properties of matter create intelligent code. The natural properties of matter bring destruction to created things. New buildings don't build themselves by the natural properties of matter. New buildings tend to rot, rust, and crumble. The natural properties of matter subject DNA to deterioration rather than improvement. **The natural properties of matter are destructive not constructive.** Evolution wants us to imagine a world that is contrary to what we see every day. We will address this again in chapter 6 when we deal with the origin of the structure in the cell. Not only does evolution propose a spontaneous development of the information in the DNA, it also has to explain the origin of the tremendous structure in the cell that is required to read the information.

Maybe you have an objection. You have heard of situations in which science has shown some mutations have been beneficial. I will refer you to Stanford's work on this matter[xxix]. He is a seasoned geneticist and deals with that matter fully. Simply put: 999 mutations out of 1000 are harmful. Those that provide some kind of advantage are only temporary helps in toxic situations. They come, like many forms of medicine, with harmful side effects. Geneticists are not overly worried about the human genome

PROVE TO ME THAT THERE IS A GOD

getting better. They are concerned about the buildup of harmful genes causing disease. The human genome is deteriorating not improving.

Application to real life:

Within the life of every man and woman of faith comes those grey days when you start to question the reality of God. I would presume that most everyone reading this book has had those days.

Maybe you're in one right now.

They happen in me as well.

It is on those days of weak faith that I remind myself about the DNA code. I remind myself that there is no known mechanism in the entire universe, within all the natural properties of matter, in which intelligent coded information spontaneously develops. The existence of the DNA code and all the mechanisms of the cell necessary to apply that code demand the existence of an intelligence source. There must be a God!

I no longer have the need for a radio preacher to demonstrate the existence of God to me. God made it known to everyone through what He has created. And my studies in biology have confirmed the reality of God. The DNA code proves beyond a shadow of doubt: someone created life! An intelligent life created all life.

Application to real life:

Point: intelligent code always originates in the mind of an intelligent being. The existence of a complex code in the bodies of every living creature demands an intelligent source. DNA is the Code of God.

FOUNDATION FIVE

How long ago?

How much time since the beginning…
How old is the earth?

4.5 billion years old
OR
6,500 years old?

FIVE

THE PROBLEM OF LIGHT AND TIME

"If the earth is less than 10,000 years old, as you creationists claim, how do you explain the fact that we see light from stars that are billions of light-years away? The universe would have to be in existence for billions of years for light to travel across space and reach the earth ... I am waiting for an answer."

DR. AGNOSTIC

O n the first day of creation, God began rotating the earth setting the day/night cycle in motion. He also created visible light as a form of energy. The source of that light is not stated in the text. A clue that may uncover the source of this light is discovered near the end of the Bible; the book of Revelation speaks of a New Heavens and a New Earth that will replace the existing universe. Notice the source of light for that future world:

Revelation 21:23 (NIV84)

23   The city does not need the sun or the moon to shine on it, for the glory of God gives it light, and the Lamb is its lamp.

This New Heavens and New Earth do not have the sun as its source of light. The source of light is from God himself and *this would have to be the case*. This new universe will be eternal. It will demand a candle (stars) that will never burn out. Many Bible expositors, including myself, conclude that the light source for the first three days of creation is the same source as the final one we see in Revelation 21:23. The source is God himself. That idea alone will not solve the time-light problem. Let's look at day four of creation to identify the problem fully:

Day Four, The Stellar Universe

Genesis 1:14–19 (NIV84)

14   And God said, "Let there be lights in the expanse of the sky to separate the day from the night, and let them serve as signs to mark seasons and days and years, 15 and let them be lights in the expanse of the sky to give light on the earth." And it was so. 16 God made two great lights—the greater light to govern the day and the lesser light to govern the night. He also made the stars. 17 God set them in the expanse of the sky to give light on the earth, 18 to govern the day and the night, and to separate light from darkness. And God saw that it was good. 19 And there was evening, and there was morning—the fourth day.

Lights are placed in the sky and the word "expanse" is stated again. In this text, we gain an increased certainty that the expanse is outer space. This is made clear since the stars are placed in the expanse.

Does the word "expanse" imply that space is expanding? By itself it is insufficient. There are 17 verses in the Old Testament that present the idea that the expanse is expanding. Consider Psalm 104:

Psalm 104:1–2 (NIV84)

1   Praise the Lord, O my soul. O Lord my God, you are very great; you are clothed with splendor and majesty.

2   He wraps himself in light as with a garment [source of light in verse 3;] he stretches out the heavens like a tent [the expanding universe]

In Psalm 104 we uncover a description of God stretching out the heavens. Also see Isaiah 40:20, Jeremiah 10:12 and Zechariah 12:1 as further examples. This expanding of the universe is an important concept in the time-space problem.[xxx]

In Genesis 1:16 Biblical writer has taken the perspective of someone who is looking up into the sky from the Earth's surface and the stars appear in the heavens. On day four, light from the stars, moon, and sun reached the Earth. The text states that on the fourth day, God called into existence these stellar bodies; however, some argue that they were created on day one and that the light from the stellar bodies does not reach the planet's surface until day four. The Hebrew text is quite clear that God spoke and then created the stellar universe all on the fourth day. The text uses the standard sequence, "Let there be lights … and God made the lights … and God set them in the expanse of the heavens." This formation of the stellar bodies within the "expanse" may be the calling into existence of additional matter or, more likely, the starting of the nuclear reactions within the stars, essentially "lighting the candles" in space.

This timing of the light reaching the Earth's surface on the fourth day is problematic. As noted earlier, this is problematic since many of the stars are millions of light years away. This would imply that the light we see in the sky each night has taken millions of years to reach our planet. How can we reconcile a young creation and the starlight visible in our night skies? Let's work though the issues:

It seems apparent by the order of creation that God wished to demonstrate that He created the Earth as a special place. The first through third creation days focus upon the development of the Earth. Christian geologists love to look at the basement layers of rocks and consider that these are likely from those first two to three days of creation when God was developing the planet core, mantle, and crust. The crust was a particular focus of day three with dry land appearing. On the fourth day, God sets the stellar universe in motion placing the Earth in its location within our galaxy and its precise distance from our star, the sun.

This brings us to an important juncture in how we see the Earth relative to the universe. The focus of the Bible is not the stellar universe. The focus of the Bible is the Earth, this amazing and beautiful planet. The Bible presents the universe as support to the Earth.

Many scientists today, however, take a different view. They look out in the vast stellar universe marveling at its complex galaxies. When their eyes then return to this Earth, it appears as a tiny insignificant speck,

one of billions and billions of such specks. They postulate that when the Big Bang occurred, the Earth was just one of the specks of dust among millions and billions. It is just by chance that this globe is the perfectly correct distance from the sun, that it has a tilt on its axis to give us seasons, and that it rotates in precisely 24 hours to make it hospitable for life. By this unsettling reasoning, since there are potentially billions upon billions of planets, it is simply a matter of mathematics and chance that brought about the precision needed for life to exist on this planet. By this view, Earth is not special. Earth is just an accident that chance brought to play. This view envisions the universe giving birth to the Earth. I call this idea unsettling since it removes intentionality by someone greater than us. This is unsettling since it then implies that human life is of no real significance. We will delve into the idea of value of human life in much greater detail in chapters to come.

I make the case that the Earth is, in fact, extremely special. Everything about this planet sets it apart from the other planets in our solar system and beyond. The high amount of water on this planet that is in liquid state, the atmosphere being just right to support life, the magnetic field and atmospheric gases that protect the Earth from the sun's dangerous radiation, and even the moon rotating around the Earth make this planet appear to be specially created; this planet is finely tuned for life to exist. This is the scenario the Bible presents.

As I have studied the Bible, particularly the first couple of verses, and found that it is astonishing in its implications and accuracy to all that we see relative to time and space, I have grown to trust the Scriptures and its accuracy. Given the trustworthiness of the Scriptures, I conclude that we are best in seeing that God created the Earth as a special place. He formed matter and placed it in space which began time. He cast light upon the Earth and started the 24-hour rotation cycle giving us even temperatures and measurement of time. He took the first three days of creation carefully forming this planet and forming the plant kingdom on its surface.

So it's at this point you'll have to make a choice. Is the Earth special? The Bible says it is. If you let the Bible simply speak and not try to reshape its words, its ideas, to match the ideas of current scientific theories, you will conclude that God began His work on Earth in a special way.

That being the case, the Earth was specially created by God for life. I interpret this fourth day to mean that the stellar universe was created on the fourth day for the purpose of shedding its light upon the Earth. Underlying my interpretation is the presupposition that God was there when the universe began. His description of those events would be the only accurate description available to humankind. *Since He was there, His description of the events would be the only one that is perfectly correct.*

This opens the door to delve into how Moses knew about the events of Creation since Genesis is his writings. We have a human author. How did he know these things? This brings us to the issue of inspiration of the Biblical text. The original writings by Moses had to be inspired. How did that happen? The Bible claims to be written by men to whom God revealed specific ideas. Let me define that as Revelation. God placed into the minds of specific people His very thoughts. These people are then called prophets. When they convey the ideas from God in writing, we call the words as inspired. When people carefully evaluate the resultant words, they discover that the personality of the prophet is conveyed in the words. A discerning person can recognize the writings of the apostle Paul as opposed to the apostle Peter. Both are prophets whose words are inspired because God revealed His ideas to them. Here is a statement that defines inspiration:

> God so directed the human authors of the Scriptures that without destroying their individuality, personal interest, or literary style, His complete thought toward man was recorded without error in the words of the original manuscripts.

The Bible claims that the words of Moses were inspired. Jesus quoted from Moses more than any other prophet of the Old Testament of the Bible, recognizing him as a prophet. Therefore, God gave Moses the concepts that he then recorded in the Hebrew language. His writings were inspired to the level that God oversaw the final product so that it was exactly as He wanted it to be, word for word exactly as God intended it to be. Our English bibles are translations of the original Hebrew. Therefore, quality bible teaching takes into account the meanings of the original Hebrew language. The bible-believing Christian believes that the original Hebrew text contains a perfect communication from the Creator and Genesis is the record of the Creation. No man could have had access to what is recorded here unless God took the initiative to reveal it to us, recording the events through inspired text. Now let me repeat my conclusions about what we have in Genesis chapter 1: *since God was there, His description of the events would be the only one that is perfectly correct.*

With that background, we need to return to our original problem: starlight and time. We now have good reasons from solid observations of our universe to conclude that many of the stars and galaxies are millions, even billions of light-years away from the Earth. That means that the light generated by the most distant stars would have traveled millions of years before reaching the Earth. If the Earth is only 6,500 to 7,000 years old, how is it possible that we can see light from stars that are millions, even billions, of light-years away? This is a great and challenging question. When I first began to investigate this in the 1980s we really had no answers. Some speculated that there were light trails (of some sort) that God created so the light could reach the Earth immediately. Others speculated that there were variations in speed of light. This latter solution seems the most untenable since the speed of light is apparently fixed by the media of space.

In 1994 Dr. D. Russell Humphreys wrote a book called *Starlight and Time* which was a totally different way of looking at this problem. His basic premise is based upon changes in **time** relative to the density of matter. This idea originates with Einstein's *Theory of Relativity* and it does have a fair amount of evidence authenticating its validity. Let me quote from his book to help you understand the basis of his idea:

Gravity Distorts Time

Let me first briefly outline where I am heading. The theory [of Dr. Humphrey's] utilizes Einstein's general theory of relativity, which is the best theory of gravity we have today. General relativity (GR) has been well-established experimentally, and is the physics framework for all modern cosmologies.

According to GR, *gravity affects time*. Clocks at low altitude should tick more slowly than clocks at a high altitude—and observations confirm this affect, which some call *gravitational time dilation...*

For example, anatomic clock at the Royal Observatory in Greenwich, England, tics 5 µs per year slower than an identical clock at the national Bureau of standards in Boulder, Colorado, both clocks being accurate to about 1 µs per year. The difference is exactly what general relativity predicts for a one-mile difference in altitude.[xxxi]

To put this very simplistically, time is distorted by density of matter and, therefore, does not tick at the same rate evenly throughout the universe. This is known to be true and has been experimentally confirmed as cited above. But it is not known how significant this affects time today. It all depends on assumptions about the uniformity of matter in the universe and how it all originated. In other words, we know time is not uniform at different places in the universe. We just are not certain how significant this is. That idea alone should be a warning to us. We understand that time is not uniform, but we act as though we know it is.

With that introduction let me explain this fourth solution a little more:

Expanding Universe in the early days of Creation

Matter is more dense in the center of the universe. Here, time would run the slowest

Matter is less dense in the edges of the expanding universe. Here, time would run extremely fast compared to the center

In the early days of creation as the universe was expanding into hyperspace (a theorized additional dimension), there would exist a great differential in time throughout the universe. This differential in time occurs because the mass of the universe would be greatest in the center of the universe. (This view assumes that there would be a definite center). The mass difference found in the center of the universe (where it would be the densest) to the outer fringes (where it would be less dense) would be the most extreme in the early days of the expanding universe. The closer to the center of the universe a planet is, the slower time would pass in relationship to other planets and stars located much more distant from the center of the mass of the universe. In this scenario, billions of years may pass in the distant galaxies while only days pass on Earth. Since the Bible is presenting the creation story from the perspective of the surface of the Earth, minutes to days may go by on Earth while billions of years pass near the ends of the universe. This differential of time offers a possible explanation for how light from distant galaxies could be visible on a young Earth.

In the years to come there will be many brilliant attempts to solve this puzzle. But there is an underlying issue that must be considered. We are assuming that we truly know how time behaves in outer space. That is a no small assumption. We really do not know much about how time and space work together. Consider this: we sit on a little speck of dust called the Earth and look out at a universe that is gigantic. From this perspective, we are asserting with great confidence that millions of years must pass in order to get the light from distant stars to our planet. Yet none of us has been past the moon! Our probes have only gone to the most distant planet in our solar system. *We simply do not have much knowledge about how time in space works.*

Let me give you an example that may prove helpful with this issue of time and space. If you take my weight by using a common bathroom scale while I am standing on planet Earth, it will be somewhere around 220 pounds. But if you take my weight by using the same bathroom scale on the moon I will only weigh 37 pounds. The reason for the change is that the gravity on the moon is 1/6 of that on Earth so the push of my body weight down upon the springs of the scale will be 1/6 of that on Earth. The reason that there is such a difference is that the conditions on the moon are dramatically different from those on the Earth. The method of measuring our *weight* is simply not designed for accurate use outside our planet.

In contrast, if we measure *mass* (not weight) we use a *balance*. The balance does not use springs that compress to measure our weight. Rather, it uses a beam with iron weights that are pulled by the gravity. In this case, the force of gravity is pulling on the weights and the person equally. This method of measurement is designed to work in differing conditions on or off this planet. Therefore, my mass, which is about 100 kilograms on Earth, will be 100 kilograms on the moon when measured on a balance. That means that measurement of mass (unlike measuring weight) is suited for varying situations. For further consideration of these ideas of time measurements in space, see Mark Amunrud's web page www.amunrud.com.

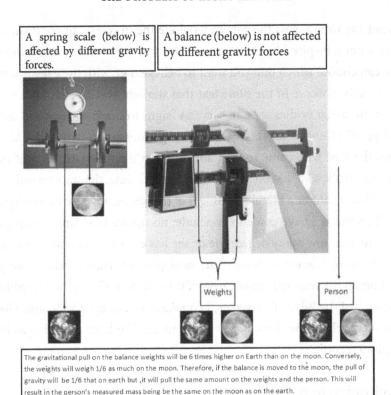

A spring scale (below) is affected by different gravity forces.	A balance (below) is not affected by different gravity forces

The gravitational pull on the balance weights will be 6 times higher on Earth than on the moon. Conversely, the weights will weigh 1/6 as much on the moon. Therefore, if the balance is moved to the moon, the pull of gravity will be 1/6 that on earth but ,it will pull the same amount on the weights and the person. This will result in the person's measured mass being be the same on the moon as on the earth.

This brings me to the point: time, as we understand it, is measured on the Earth and all our methods of measuring it are relative to the Earth (like weight). We do not have an adequate and proven means of measuring time in deep space (like mass). What seems obvious on Earth can be drastically in error in deep space (like thinking I will weigh 220 lbs. on the moon). It is unwise to assert that the Bible is in serious error because our assumptions on time and space seem to indicate so. In really, _we cannot be certain how time worked in the past when we try to measure it from the Earth relative to deep space._

So here's your answer Dr. Agnostic and all others: be careful when you hear that the Bible is in serious error with science because of time and distances in space. None of us was there at creation and _none of us has even been beyond our moon._ We do not have an accurate method of measuring time across the galaxy, let alone the universe. In contrast, we have a book inspired by the Creator Who was there and is everywhere. You can choose which one you want to believe. I go with the eyewitness.

Finally, observe in the Bible text that starlight was created for a purpose: the stellar bodies were to serve as "signs to mark seasons and days and years" (Genesis 1:14). One interesting observation is that the Magi from the East who came to visit and worship the newborn King of the Jews were following a star (Matthew 2:2). In this case, the stars served as a sign. That would be a literal fulfillment of this stated purpose for starlight.

This much I have come to conclude: no matter how smart a person is, no matter how many degrees he or she has earned, no matter what the consensus of science is, none of us were present when creation began. No human has traveled the vastness of the universe. Given the incredible accuracy of the Bible's first verses, I conclude we can trust its words. God was there. He knows how it was really made. We have the Bible as his inspired record.

Application to real life:

POINT: since we have no reliable means of measuring time across the universe, it is foolish to claim that science has proved the Bible wrong about time and the age of the Earth.

FOUNDATION SIX

Life

How did it begin?

Life came about by the basic properties of matter
over a long period of time
OR
Someone made life

ORIGIN OF LIFE: A GIANT LEAP
OF FAITH

With his father's notes in hand, Indiana Jones (Referencing the Hollywood movie: *Indiana Jones and the Last Crusade*) had overcome two major near-lethal challenges to rescue his father who was shot in the abdomen by the evil antagonist. His father's only chance lies across a chasm where the challis of Christ has been hidden since the Crusades. This challis had fictional miraculous healing powers that alone could save a man from the soon-to-be-fatal gunshot wound. No man has succeeded in retrieving the challis. With success over two challenges behind him, the third and last challenge appeared to be impossible. Before him lay a giant chasm descending thousands of feet to the valley floor. Across the chasm was the door to where the chalice of Christ would be found. No bridge was to be seen. To step out would be sheer madness.

Reading his father's notes, Indy quickly realized that this last challenge was a leap of faith. He must step out in faith … he must step out into thin air … to certain death. Sweat beads up on his forehead. His face grimaces. There are no other options. But who would just step out into a canyon, into thin air, to certain death? There is a pause as Indy considers what he is expected to do. The film flashes back to his father who lies on the floor of the cold cave, dying from the wound. He cries out in pain, as his friends shout, "Hurry, Indy! You must hurry!" He must step out into the chasm, to certain death; in faith he must believe that somehow, he will make it to the other side.

If you have seen the movie, you will know that there is a secret bridge that is so well camouflaged you cannot see it from above. Indiana Jones  steps out in the great leap of faith only to find that there was no real danger at all.

As we enter in to the ideas of origins, we will be faced with a crossroads of faith. Did life begin by itself from raw materials that spontaneously came together? Or did life have some outside force or mind or spirit who injected information and design into this world? How can we come to any sane and rational conclusion? With the issue of origins, we are forced to step out in faith. Faith in molecules that spontaneously brought about the first living cell or faith in a spirit or God who designed life. Because we are researching something in distant history, it always contains an element of faith.

A rational person in the twenty-first century must determine the trustworthy nature of the person who is presenting the ideas that will be either accepted *in faith* or rejected *in faith*. Whatever view you take, understand that it will demand an element of faith!

Let me explain: Those who believe in evolution cannot cite anyone who has observed the beginning of life processes. Therefore, belief in evolution is based upon the evidence after-the-fact and requires an element of faith that the events leading to the formation of the first life form will be worked out by people. Even when ideas about evolution seem to work, a person is still required to take a leap of faith in the researchers' conclusions. No one was there. Not a single living thing was alive to record the events. It will always be a leap of faith.

This also brings up an important issue: science is always in a state of advancement. In advancement, old ideas that we thought were true are discarded and replaced with new ones as investigation progresses. This means that ultimately, faith in evolution is not rooted in the current understanding of evolution but rather that someday humans will find a way to uncover the actual way in which life arose from nonlife. *To believe in evolution is not so much a belief in the present day understanding of evolution, but rather that the concept is true even if our present understanding of it is wrong.*

For those who believe the Bible, they are trusting that the Bible is inspired by God and this God is trustworthy. With is this view, biblical Christians believe that God was there and He is the One who designed life. This is a leap of faith in the person of God and the trustworthy nature of the historical record He gives to humanity. This leap of faith assumes that: 1) God exists. 2) He took the initiative to communicate with His created people. 3) The Bible is a record of that communication that originated with God and given to humans [by inspiration] to record in written words. 4) That original ancient record has been preserved through the ages of human history. This is the deeply convinced and held view of the author.

If the above is true, then we conveniently have a written record from someone Who was present in the beginning. Studies of the record (the Bible) will be of tremendous aid in the pursuit of truth.

Having defined the issues of faith, that there exists a leap of faith in either direction (evolution or creation), which direction contains the best evidence?

Let's look, for a moment, at what the Bible says about the evidence relative to this decision. Within these words of the Bible, we discover that it claims that there exists tremendous evidence for a Creator that would have to be intentionally overlooked for any serious researcher to miss:

Romans 1:19–20 (NIV84)
19 since what may be known about God is plain to them [people who reject God], because God has made it plain to them.
20 For since the creation of the world God's invisible qualities—his eternal power and divine nature—have been clearly seen, being understood from what has been made, so that men are without excuse.

The point here is that the leap of faith that God is expecting of humanity is as "plain as the nose on your face." The creation makes it clear that He exists. All around us are marvelous living creatures. The mere existence of complex life forms on Earth, the Bible is claiming, demands a Creator.

I OBJECT:

Many people today, maybe you, object. You would really like to know for certain that a Creator exists. But when it comes to faith in God, you feel like Indiana Jones stepping out to certain death because your five senses have clearly identified the danger. You may have been taught that evolution is a fact. Maybe you have read works like Richard Dawkins' *The Selfish Gene*, in which he states, "Today the theory of evolution is about as much open to doubt as the theory that the Earth goes around the sun, but the full implications of Darwin's revolution have yet to be widely realized."xxxii Therefore, anyone who has a reasonable amount of education knows this to be reality. Science, it appears to many, has essentially made it clear that faith in God is optional since the natural properties of matter have been proven to have brought about life spontaneously. So when the Bible is taught, or a preacher comes along and challenges you to believe in Jesus, you wonder if you are simply stepping out into nothing. I have also observed that many of those who object would truly like to know for sure if life is simply the product of time and chance or it is the product of a God who brought it all into existence. There always lies some lingering doubt in the truest of believers in evolution. To that end we will proceed.

We studied, in chapter three, different approaches to the interpretation of the book of Genesis. The first is a literal approach. Those who take this approach believe that God literally created the universe, the world, and all the plant and animal life, including humans, in six literal 24-hour days. In response to the scientific revolution that began in the latter part of the nineteenth century, many people have turned to variations of a *Theistic Evolutionary* approach to Bible interpretation. In the *Theistic Evolutionary* approach, people believe, **by faith**, that God used evolution to create life on this planet. Undergirding this approach are variations of the *Day-Age theory*. Recall that in the *Day-Age theory*, each of the days of creation in Genesis chapter one represent, possibly, millions of years of evolutionary processes. For those of you who are favoring this approach, I'm afraid to tell you in advance ... there lies ahead some bad news. When you look carefully at the fifth and sixth days of creation, you will discover that they simply will not comply with evolutionary concepts as we are taught today.

In these last two days of creation, the Bible describes God creating all the animal life that we see on planet Earth. In each of these days God speaks, and the animal life forms come forth upon the planet.

In contrast, science has proposed a different scenario. In this modern-day scientific scenario, all the life that teams in the oceans, all the birds that fly across the heavens, all the animals that charge forth across the prairie, and even the worms that burrow through the soil are the product of chance. This magnificent scientific story begins with certain chemicals that came together by chance, organizing themselves into extremely complex chemical microstructures.

Before we move on to the biblical view, it is crucial that we look at this opposing view.

Origin of Life - What It Takes

Darwinian Evolution informs us that life spontaneously arose on this Earth maybe some 3.8 billion years ago[xxxiii]. Remember, no one was there. It was simply chemicals that spontaneously worked together to produce life. I am always amazed when I read such statements in biology books, museums, or web sites. I am amazed at two things:

1. The dazzling amount of faith it takes to make that statement
2. The boldness in which it is stated

Two serious problems impede belief by any open-minded person in evolution. These are the origin of the information (discussed in chapter 4) and the origin of the structural designs in the living cell (discussed below). These two ideas are deal breakers for me to ever return to a Darwinian belief. Let me show you why:

In chapter 4, I introduced you to the complexity of the DNA code that is required by each of our cells to direct life functions. We are told by Darwinian evolution that this code "made itself" by accident and without a code designer[xxxiv]. That is a monumental leap of faith. But there is much more. The code is worthless without a tremendously complex system of microscopic structures that translate that code to function. Here is a simple formula for life:

[DNA + Structures + Energy] = life.

In this formula, the brackets [ ] symbolize the cell membrane that is needed to protect the structures. In order for you to grasp the level of leap of faith that evolution is expecting of you, I am going to take you on a *very simplified* journey into the daily functions of the simplest life form: the living cell.

Some time ago, my family and I toured the Boeing 787 production plant in Everett, WA. We walked through the world's largest building. It contains at least 472 million cubic feet. In this plant, they were assembling one of the world's most complex airplanes. When the complexity of this aircraft is compared to the immensely greater (compressed/microscopic) complexity of the simplest bacteria cell, I marvel at the faith of the scientists who believe it all happened by accident. Nothing in that Boeing building was by chance. Everything was by careful design. To fail in any aspect could spell great aeronautical disaster.

In my studies of biology and biochemistry, I have come to understand that life is made up of extremely complex chemical reactions in very controlled environments. I have come to conclude that even the simplest single cell organism is far more complex than the product of a large manufacturing plant, even that of the latest Boeing aircraft.

> The icons below will help us keep track of what processes are going on in the living cell. Each Icon will represent a certain "organelle" in the cell that has specific function. In the first case below I am using power lines to represent the cell's power generation organelle called "mitochondria."

Power: The cells of any living organism contain complex miniaturized machines and structures to power them. In the same manner as the Boeing plant, the living cell must have a power source. The Boeing plant had numerous high  voltage lines entering the plant bringing power from a distant source. In the microscopic cell, the power generators are within the cell. These tiny power plants are called *mitochondria*.

Manufacturing: All cells also contain their own manufacturing centers or factories. These are called *ribosomes*. These factories must have blueprints of the products they are to make.

Detailed Blueprints: In the cell, the *DNA* contains the coded blueprints. It contains the code that will be translated by the ribosomes into precise manufactured products such as proteins. The cell's DNA is a literal library of microscopic chemical blueprints that store technical specifications of the particular proteins that the cell is required to produce. The specific protein products are precisely detailed and specific to the particular species to which the cell belongs.

Blueprint Copies: The information, described above is contained on a chemical molecule (the DNA) that very precisely copies itself when the cell divides. That way the information is carried to each of the daughter cells without any loss. (When a cell divides, the two resultant cells are called "daughter cells"). You might say that the library has a printing press to copy itself.

CPA to Check the Books: The cell even has systems to check for errors in the DNA code that may occur in the reproduction processes. This function is much like a certified public accountant doing an audit on the books. This magnificent library must be protected and able to reproduce itself accurately without any error.

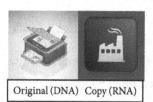

Original (DNA) Copy (RNA)

In a large manufacturing plant such as the Boeing plant, the original copies of the blueprints for an aircraft are kept somewhere safe. Today, we keep electronic copies offsite (in the cloud, redundant hard drives). These copies are kept off premises in case of a fire or accident. Massive amounts of money have been spent on these detailed blueprint drawings. The originals must be kept safe so only copies are sent out on the manufacturing floor.

Similarly in the cell, the original blueprints (the DNA) are kept safe in the cell nucleus. Only copies *(RNA)* are allowed out to the manufacturing centers (the manufacturing centers of the cell are called ribosomes). The cell has a photocopy-like process that keeps the originals in the safety of the nucleus while the copies go out to the ribosomes (the factory floor). The process of photocopying the DNA produces a copy called RNA. DNA contains an immense code. It contains all the needed information to make over 3,000 different proteins for a simple single-cell lifeform to exist. The code is immensely more complex in multicellular organisms like people. However, the photocopy system does not copy the entire DNA. Rather, it copies the needed portion of the code to make a particular protein. It has systems in place to know how much of the code should be copied for a particular protein. It is only the copy of that part of the code (the RNA) that leaves the nucleus (the library of the cell) to be used on the manufacturing floor (the ribosomes).

At the ribosomes (the factories), the code on the RNA is translated into a construction sequence of chemicals (amino acids). The completed products bend and shape themselves naturally by chemical forces on the molecule, taking the shape of the required protein. This is all happens because of the atomic level electromagnetic forces in play caused by the sequence of amino acids; all of this happens because of the code.

Look at the drawing of the living cell below. I have added the icons to help you equate the structure with its function. When you consider the complexity of the cell and its microscopic size, it leaves a person marveling at life. This is why I love the study of biology! It is truly amazing.

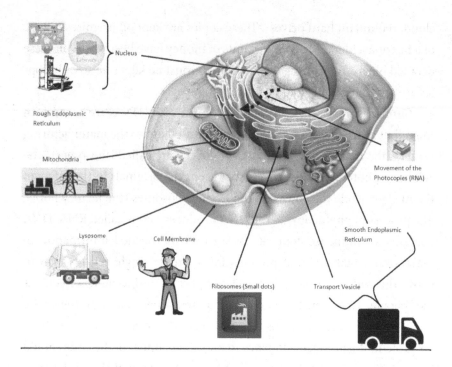

Once a product is made, it must be packaged and labeled so that when it is shipped, it will arrive at the appropriate place. Within the cell, this is accomplished in an area called the endoplasmic reticulum and the Golgi apparatus (the shipping department).

The cell also has waste products in the process of manufacturing that must be disposed of appropriately; this is accomplished by the lysosomes, the garbage disposal system of the cell.

All of this must be done within the safety of the cell membrane, which functions to keep deadly chemicals out and allow the specific products needed by the cell in. It acts like the police force. The cell membrane is in itself quite complex. It contains specific sites (pores) that act as security gates to only allow certain products into the cell.

For a simple bacterium to exist, it must be able to produce over 3,000 complex proteins.[xxxv] Proteins are made up of building blocks called amino acids. These amino acids, of which there are about twenty, must be connected together in a precise order. An average protein has a chain of 300 amino acids. Any mistakes in the order will cause the final protein to be lethal, weakened in functionality, or completely nonfunctional. The cell manufacturing center must be able to read the RNA copies of the DNA and assemble the amino acids in the precise order dictated by the DNA.

The DNA of even the simplest life forms contains all the codes necessary to build each one of the 3,000 specific proteins that the cell requires. But the code is worthless without the hardware … the manufacturing organelles found in a living cell. An analogy to this magnificent code could be this: the codes within a Widows 8 disk. A lot of information is on that disk. But here is the catch: all of that magnificent code is worthless without the computer to read it.

In the cell, the information in the DNA is worthless without the above-described cellular structures to run it. The leap of faith that Darwinian evolution is asking of you is that you believe that **both:** 1) the complex intelligent code and 2) all the needed structures of the cell came together spontaneously *and* simultaneously without any outside help. The code is of no value without the hardware, and the hardware is of no value without the code. They must develop at the same time.

Let's put this in perspective:

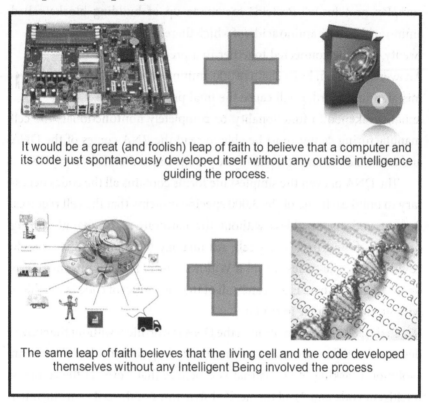

It would be a great (and foolish) leap of faith to believe that a computer and its code just spontaneously developed itself without any outside intelligence guiding the process.

The same leap of faith believes that the living cell and the code developed themselves without any Intelligent Being involved the process

Some people mock the "people of faith" (the Christians) because they believe in God as the originator of everything. They have been convinced by people like Richard Dawkins, quoted above, and others that evolution is a fact, leaving faith in God optional and essentially unnecessary. This is absolutely wrong and unscientific! *The overwhelming evidence is that faith in God is the only rational conclusion an educated person can make!* It is not a leap of faith. It is a rational faith. Belief in Darwinian evolution is a terrible leap of faith.

Life is incredibly complex. It is highly organized matter that is miniaturized beyond anything humanity has been able to produce to date. The terrible leap of faith is to believe that chemicals found in an ocean or lake in an imagined early Earth just came together by accident and created a complex code that is capable of reproducing itself. This terrible leap of faith also envisions highly complex organized structures in the living cells just accidently formed from simple chemicals.

In reality, what do we observe? Chemicals come apart over time. Chemicals do not spontaneously form highly organized structures and information. This just does not happen.

What fool would believe that if we mixed a massive pile of junk in some barrel for millions of years that it would form a functioning computer, loaded with an operating system, by accident! Why would anyone believe that chemicals formed something far more complex and it came to life?

The contrasting scenario is that what the Bible teaches. Let its words speak:

Genesis 1:20–23 (NIV84)

20 And God said, "Let the water teem with living creatures, and let birds fly above the earth across the expanse of the sky."

21 So God created the great creatures of the sea and every living and moving thing with which the water teems, according to their kinds, and every winged bird according to its kind. And God saw that it was good.

22 God blessed them and said, "Be fruitful and increase in number and fill the water in the seas, and let the birds increase on the earth."

23 And there was evening, and there was morning—the fifth day.

The biblical view of the origin of life is quite simple, though it does demand an element of faith in the person of God and His written record. The biblical view states that the source of the information in the DNA molecules and *all the manufacturing structures* that make up the different species of animal and plant life on this planet originate from an intelligence source (God). Rather than believing that time, chance, and some mechanism (unknown to us) created all the information that is coded into the smallest and most compact package we know of, the Bible says God is the source of that information and the structures needed to put that information into action.

Maybe today this book finds itself in the hands of someone who has always believed in the modern-day faith of evolutionary biology. I challenge you to reconsider all you know about life. Consider what you know about the complexity of life. Consider all you know about chemistry. Consider all you know about how information comes into existence. After you've considered all of these, ask yourself which person is the truly rational and wise person of faith: the man who believes it all happened by chance or the man who believes someone made this?

> The leap of faith that Darwinian evolution is asking of you is that you believe that both the complex intelligent code and all the needed structures of the cell came together spontaneously without any outside help.

Returning to the text, I want to call your attention that when God created the animal life, He created them according to "kinds." Once you leave behind an evolutionary paradigm, you can see that this reflects exactly what can be observed in the physical world. There are dog kinds like we looked at earlier. There are the horse "kinds" which include the zebra, donkey, and horses. The cat kind includes domestic cats, bobcats, lynx, and lions.

Notice the awesome blessing by God, following the creation of animal life:

Genesis 1:22 (NIV84)

God blessed them and said, "Be fruitful and increase in number and fill the water in the seas, and let the birds increase on the earth."

Unlike plant life, God blesses animal life. He blesses both the fish and the birds. He is blessing them with reproductive success so that their numbers increase across the face of the earth.

A final important observation from this text is that aquatic life and avian life were created on the same day. Later it will be discussed that amphibians and terrestrial animals are created on the sixth day. This is a serious problem for evolutionary *Day-Age* theorist in that birds are created before amphibians. According to the evolutionary scenario, the order is wrong! If you are going to try and use the *Day-Age* theory along with theistic evolution as the basis of your beliefs in the Bible, please see clearly that God got it wrong. He says in the Bible that the birds were made before the amphibians. That would mean millions of years (represented in this theory in each of the biblical days) of fish and bird life would have to pass before the amphibians have their time. Evolutionary theory describes millions of years of amphibians and reptiles eventually evolving into the birds. The same holds true for whales. These are great creatures of the sea that God states were created on day 5. Yet scientists classify them as mammals since they produce milk for their young. Evolution proposes that some land animal (created on day 6) began living near the sea-land interface eventually evolving into the whale. That story is one of great faith in evolution! The point here is that God states that whales were

> Who got it wrong?
> God or man?
> Either God created the birds before the amphibians and evolution has it wrong,
> or
> the birds did evolve from reptiles and God got it wrong.

created on day 5, before the land animals were created. Finally, the stellar universe was created on day 4, not preday 1. These order issues cause tremendous difficulty for a naturalistic approach to Genesis one and evolutionary Day-Age Theory.

Here is the faith challenge referred to earlier: either God actually created the birds before the amphibians and evolution has it wrong, or the birds did evolve from reptiles and God got it wrong. You cannot prove either answer in a scientific lab. It happened in the past and there is no definitive means of proving either view.

The arrival of land animals:

Genesis 1:24–25 (NIV84)

24 And God said, "Let the land produce living creatures according to their kinds: livestock, creatures that move along the ground, and wild animals, each according to its kind." And it was so.

25 God made the wild animals according to their kinds, the livestock according to their kinds, and all the creatures that move along the ground according to their kinds. And God saw that it was good.

The Bible now describes God's creative process in making land animals described in three major groups as they relate to humankind. In taxonomy (the classification of animals), scientists appropriately use anatomical similarities to classify life. For instance, animals are divided into the subphylum Vertebra. Animals in this group have backbones. Anatomical classification is helpful. God groups animals as well. He groups them according to how they relate to people.

The first group is **livestock**. I recommend that when you think of the word "livestock," you think of the word "domestic." These are animals that can live in close proximity to humans.

When I was in veterinary practice, I occasionally was called upon to help owners of bobcats. Predictably, bobcat owners can be detected the moment they walk into the clinic… by the bandages or the scars on their arms. The very nature of bobcats makes them questionable pets. On the other hand, cows will not make good pets either, but they can live in close proximity to and be managed by humans with a certain amount of care. I would define "livestock" as animals that have a *mental nature* that is compatible with existing close to human beings.

The next group is **"creatures that move along the ground,"** including everything from worms to snakes to rodents. The last group consists of **"wild animals,"** including all animals that are not compatible with living close to human beings (lions, rhinoceros, antelope, and other wildlife). These animals need lots of space and do not function as well with fences and corrals.

These animals were created according to their kind, much like the fish, the birds, and all the plant life. God saw that His creation of these animals was good.

There was one more creature that needs to be made on the sixth day. This creature changes everything. We will consider that one in the next chapter.

Application to real life:

Q: Can you prove to me that God exists?

A: I do not need to. The creation provides the evidence if you have the open mind to see it. The living cell is far more complex than any manufacturing plant people have built and it is microscopic. Life shouts out, "Someone had to make this!"

Q: Why cannot I believe that God used evolution to create life?

A: The order of creation of birds and amphibians is directly opposite of that predicted by evolution. In other words, the evolutionary order of origins of birds is that amphibians came first and then millions of years of evolution brought forth birds. The Bible states that God created the bird *before* the amphibians. Either evolution got it wrong or God did. I vote God got it right.

PART TWO

HUMAN LIFE

FOUNDATION SEVEN

What is the value of your life?

People ... just what makes humanity special?

<u>Let me clarify what is at stake with this question:</u>

Human life is of grand value. That is good.
OR
Life has no purpose or meaning.... That is a real downer.

SEVEN

WHAT MAKES YOU SO SPECIAL?

From *USA Today*, July 26, 1988

Services are today (July 26, 1988) in New York for Carter Cooper, 23, son of Gloria Vanderbilt, who jumped to his death Friday. Vanderbilt, 64, great-great granddaughter of railroad and shipping magnate Cornelius Vanderbilt, was in seclusion Monday after the tragedy.

Cooper jumped from the 14th floor terrace of his mother's Manhattan apartment. Police say his mother was trying to talk him out of it when he pushed off from a ledge. Friends say he was disconsolate after breaking up with a girlfriend months ago.

Friday afternoon, Cooper went to his mother's penthouse apartment to have lunch with her, according to police. After taking a nap, Cooper reportedly stumbled into his mother's bedroom, muttering "What's it all about?" Then he ran to her terrace.

Vanderbilt was trying to restrain him when he jumped.

What is it all about?

What is life, specifically human life, all about?

In 1999, which health problem killed more young people (aged 15 to 24) than cancer, heart disease, AIDS, birth defects, stroke, and chronic lung disease combined? According to the National Center for Injury Prevention and Control, the answer is suicide. Also, according to the National Center for Health Statistics, suicide was the leading cause of death among both 10- to 14-year-olds and 15- to 19-year-olds in 2000.[xxxvi]

According to a 1999 Gallup survey of teens, 47 percent of American teens personally know someone who has attempted suicide; 37 percent have discussed suicide with friends; 25 percent have considered it themselves, with 9 percent coming close to committing suicide.

Does it really matter if a person takes his or her life?

What is the basis of your decision?

Many years ago, I was asked to speak at a pro-life rally. I stepped up to the podium and the crowd grew silent to listen to the words of their guest speaker. I began by saying these words:

"Good evening. My name is Dr. Kevin Horton and I routinely perform abortions in my medical practice. Not only do I perform abortions, but I also prescribe medications for the purpose of procuring abortions. It is not uncommon for me to perform hysterectomies on pregnant patients. This essentially aborts the young."

I was about to face a riot. This was a pro-life rally and here was a medical practitioner who performed abortions standing in front of them and had no ethical hesitations in stating his affirmation of abortion. I relieved the tension when I informed them that I am a veterinarian, and my patients are animals. Some in the crowd, and maybe some reading this, are bothered by my apparent callous approach to animal life. Please excuse that for the moment. It is not that I am so callous about animal life; after all, I dedicated my earliest productive years to the preservation and aid of the health of animals. Yet, in the arena of ethics it is important that we all look carefully at the ideas of medicine and its role in abortion and euthanasia. Veterinarians have a distinct and appropriate ethic when it comes to these life-and-death issues.

The laws in nearly every society provide a special protection to human life as opposed to animal life. There exists an apparent universal understanding that human life carries some kind of intrinsic value that is above the value of animal life. When a government or entity devalues a certain population of people, we call these crimes against humanity and declare that entity to be evil. What is the basis of this declaration? It is answered in the question of what it means to be human.

This leads to the question: why are the ethics applied by veterinary practitioners on their patients different from the ethics applied by physicians on their patients? The answer to this question relates to *the value of the patients*. There is a different value placed upon a human child against that of a calf or a kitten. Since the famous Roe vs. Wade decision of the Supreme Court of the United States in 1973, a new ethic has been emerging in the American medical culture. This ethic blends the traditional ethics of a veterinarian relative to his or her patients with the ethics of human medicine. Abortion is now mandated legal throughout America and euthanasia is now legal in many states. This leads to tremendous ethical questions relative to human life.

> This begs the question: why are the ethics applied by veterinary practitioners on their patients different from the ethics applied by physicians on their patients?

How can a person wade through the possible solutions to this ethical quagmire?

One solid source for understanding the value of human life is the Bible. Since God is the Creator of both animal and human life, He would be the best source for navigating these ethical questions. Let's see what the Bible can tell us in working through the ethics of being human. I am quoting from the first chapter of the Bible as it relates to the sixth day of creation. On this day, God created humanity:

Genesis 1:26–27 (NIV84)

26 Then God said, "Let us make man in our image, in our likeness, and let them rule over the fish of the sea and the birds of the air, over the livestock, over all the earth, and over all the creatures that move along the ground."

27 So God created man in his own image,
in the image of God he created him;
male and female he created them.

More than one God?

First: observe that a plural pronoun "us" is used in the sentence to represent God. Christian and Jewish spiritual leaders are adamant that their Scriptures represent God as a single being. Both would agree that their beliefs are strictly monotheistic; that is, they believe in one God, not many gods. So it is strange to find a plural pronoun used in this sentence as if two or more gods were speaking. To add to the mess, people who understand Hebrew know that the word that we translate "God" is also plural. It could be translated like this, "Then the gods said, "Let us make...." This sort of translation would be accurate to the original Hebrew but is totally contrary to the Jewish and Christian belief in a single God. We know from Deuteronomy chapter 6, for instance, that God declares himself as a single being:

Deuteronomy 6:4 (NIV84)

4 Hear, O Israel: The LORD our God, the LORD is one.

Christian theology expands upon the idea of the oneness of God. Christians say that there exists in the Old Testament evidence of plurality of persons in the single God, as we note in Genesis 1:26. But it is not until the New Testament that this concept that we call the Trinity is fully revealed.

Some Christian and Jewish theologians respond to the plurality in this verse in Genesis saying that God is speaking in the *Plurality of Majesty*. The *Plurality of Majesty* is a phrase that describes how kings would often issue a decree in the plural. The decree would state something like the following, "We hereby decree for the land...." The implication of the plural was that the king and God made the decision. The *Plurality of Majesty* is evoked by some Jewish Rabbis as to the explanation for the plural pronoun and plural name 'Gods' found in Genesis 1:27. God is the ultimate majesty and therefore speaks of Himself in the plural.

Many Christian theologians point out that this is an indication of the trinity in the Old Testament (the Jewish portion of the Bible). They also point out that the word for "one" found in Deuteronomy 6:4 (quoted above) is a word that can be used to describe a consensus. Let me give you an example of this same Hebrew word being used as "oneness in consensus":

Judges 20:8 (NIV84)

8   All the people rose as <u>one</u> man, saying....

In this text, the "one man" is a consensus of a number of people. Christian theology would interpret Deuteronomy 6:4 and the "One God" as a single God with a consensus of the three persons. He is One God made up of the three persons. I like to use water to explain this concept. Water is made up of hydrogen and oxygen and is found in three states: ice, liquid water, and vapor. Ice is water. Liquid water is water. And vapor (gas) water is water. The same holds for the trinity (tri-unity) of God. The Father is God. The Son is God. The Holy Spirit is God.

Christian theology sees indications of the Trinity in the Old Testament but it is not fully developed until God the Son comes on the earth and the mystery is fully unveiled. The advent of Jesus brings a clearer understanding of the previously veiled understanding of this plurality (Father, Son, and Holy Spirit) within the singular God essence.

Made in the Image of God

When God created mankind, He says He created us in His image, in His likeness. The repetition of two words that mean essentially the same thing (*image* and *likeness*) is a common Hebrew technique to emphasize and expand the topic. When you see this kind of repetition, understand that the text is *not* stating **two** different qualities. Rather, it is emphasizing the **one** quality stated two ways. By doing this, the text is better defining what it means to be in the image of God.

What does it mean to be an image bearer of God? How are we human beings different from animal life since we bear the image of the Creator the Universe? Does this imply that we are somehow a god? Is there some godlike character within humanity? It does not take too long to discover that humanity is quite different from the God of the Bible ... so how do we reconcile this? Please be patient as we work this all out. You will not get this fully understood until we deal with the evil in humanity and this life in chapters 9–10. We must begin with the manner in which humanity was created. This will set the groundwork for dealing with the problem of evil.

In our pursuit of defining humanity and setting up ethics, we must gain an understanding into what it means for mankind to "bear the image of God." Below I have developed a chart that lists two major categories of the attributes of God. This list is not intended to be a complete list of the attributes of God—that would take a lot greater space. This list is designed to aid us in recognizing what is different about people from the rest of created life on earth.

In the chart below, the first category are attributes called *Incommunicable Attributes*. These are attributes that God did not give to mankind when he made us image bearers of him. Many of these are simply, by definition, not possible to transfer to created agents. The second category contains *Communicable Attributes*. These attributes are what God infused into the human mind that allows us to reflect His character to the world around us.

Incommunicable Attributes	Communicable Attributes
Aseity (Self-existence)	Goodness
Immutability (Never changes)	Benevolence
Infinity (No limits)	Love
Perfection (Absolutely perfect)	Grace
Eternity (Outside of time)	Mercy
Immensity (He is everywhere)	Long-suffering
Infinite Knowledge	Righteousness
Infinite Wisdom	Justice
	Knowledge
	Wisdom

The *Incommunicable Attributes* of God are attributes that He chose not to give to mankind. The *Communicable Attributes* are part of what it means to bear the image of God. Human beings were created to demonstrate to the created universe the goodness, benevolence, long-suffering, and righteousness of God. We are designed to be men and women of justice. We were given minds that desire knowledge and the pursuit of wisdom. We love each other and much of the created life that God has put on the planet with us. *Human beings are created as free moral agents.* As such, we demonstrate these attributes of God to the world around us. Let me repeat: to be humans created in the image of God means that we are free moral agents.

My many years of working with pets and livestock have given me a workable understanding of this concept: the animal life around us *responds* to our love and care. It is not in their nature to love outright. When a dog submits to its owner's commands, it is because the dog knows that it will either face punishment for disobeying or it will receive a reward for obedience. In time, their nature adjusts to our kindness (if we are a kind owner), and soon reflects it somewhat in its behavior. Dogs begin to reflect love back toward their owner. In this manner, we are demonstrating the image of God to the creation and the creation responds. It is an amazing part of being human. We have the ability to change the harsh world around us with moral character traits such as love.

I watched my big yellow lab just yesterday wander out in the field heading toward an irrigation ditch. Both my wife and I called her back. If she gets in that irrigation ditch, she will come back a muddy mess. The old dog looked at us, and even at that distance I could see what looked like her mind thinking, judging. It was as if she were weighing out her desire to cross that irrigation ditch to chew on an old carcass versus the potential ramifications of her ignoring us. She chose the latter and received her due bath. In this example, we do observe that animals have a self-will like humans. This means that free will in and of itself is not the issue of being an image bearer. The issue is moral. For my old lab, it was not an issue of "doing the right thing." It was an issue of what he wants balanced by what it will cost him when he gets home. Animal trainers all understand this instinct and work with a system of rewards and punishment.

I know some of you who are parents are saying that the dog acted much like your children. But there is a significant difference between animal behavior and human behavior. In human relationships, there exists certain qualities like love, respect, and the ability to make decisions based on justice. Consider this example: when a big dog is capable of taking a choice meal from a smaller dog, it's not an issue of justice. It is simply an issue of "the big dog wins." In our sinfulness, we may act likewise and, in so doing, act like animals (more on this in chapter 9). The difference in human thinking becomes apparent when someone objects and exclaims, "That's not fair!" The injustice of the event is exposed by the image of God that resides in the objecting person. In another example, people may step in when one dog is bullying another. They are thereby making justice a part of the situation. For animals, justice is not in the equation. Even for people who hold evolutionary views, the major observable difference between humanity and animal life is our morality. (Ayala, 2010)

Another major aspect that separates humanity from the rest of the created universe is that humans are eternal creatures. Because we are image bearers of God, we have a soul that will continue on into eternity. Please read this quote from Revelation. I quote it not to scare you; rather, I quote it to inform you of two characteristics of being an Image Bearer of God: we are eternal beings and we are held responsible for our moral nature and how we acted in this life.

Revelation 20:11–15 (NIV84)

11 Then I saw a great white throne and him who was seated on it. Earth and sky fled from his presence, and there was no place for them.

12 And I saw the dead, great and small, standing before the throne, and books were opened. Another book was opened, which is the book of life. The dead were judged according to what they had done as recorded in the books.

13 The sea gave up the dead that were in it, and death and Hades gave up the dead that were in them, and each person was judged according to what he had done.

14 Then death and Hades were thrown into the lake of fire. The lake of fire is the second death.

15 If anyone's name was not found written in the book of life, he was thrown into the lake of fire.

All humanity are created in the image of God. As such, we are free moral agents who will live on into eternity. We will be held accountable for our actions since we are moral agents. That is good in the sense that those who would terribly harm us will be held accountable. That is right. The bad part is that each one of us will be held accountable for how we have harmed others. (Again, more on this in chapter 9.)

This is a major distinction between Judeo-Christianity and the naturalistic evolutionary view of humanity. In the naturalistic view, a person is hard-pressed to define human life as more valuable than animal life. It is because of this view becoming prominent in our culture that the ethics of our society is shifting away from the high view of humanity. Consider these words by an evolutionary philosopher, "I shall argue, however, that discrediting 'human dignity' is one of the most important implications of Darwinism, and it has consequences that people have barely begun to appreciate." (Rachels, 1990) Rachels quotes Thomas Huxley affirming these issues. Huxley was often credited as *Darwin's Bulldog* since he was a very powerful speaker and advocate of Darwin's ideas. Rachels abridges Huxley by saying, "If we are only advanced apes, what of the dignity and worth of man? We think ourselves not only different from but superior to the other creatures that inhabit the earth. All of our ethics and religion tell us this. Are we now to understand that we are no better than mere apes?"[xxxvii]

Speciesism:

As a result of the moral implication of Darwinian philosophy and the dethroning of humanity, a new term has been coined: "Speciesism" which is similar to racism in that it is acting prodigious and superior against another creature. In this case, speciesism is acting prodigious and superior against a different *species*. It is specifically applied to humans discriminating against the rights of animals. The biblical doctrine of being created in the image of God is "unqualified speciesism." This new view that devalues human life is actively and passionately replacing the biblical view of the special value of humanity in our culture.

Previously, I told you that I was a speaker at a pro-life conference many years ago and I played that little game with the audience telling them that I performed abortions, but kept from them that I was a veterinarian. Sitting in the front row were a couple of ladies who were pro-choice. After my disclosure of being a vet, I described the abortion of a horse that I performed a few weeks earlier. The foal was four months in gestation when I aborted it. The abortion was performed at the request of the owners because there was a misbreeding of that mare that could endanger the mare's life. The reason I described this abortion was to make it clear that at four months of gestation, equine fetuses have hooves and tails and all the features of being a true horse. There was no doubt in my mind that I had just killed a young horse. Both would have perished without the abortion. My point here was to make sure everybody understood that in abortion of a human fetus, there is no doubt that you are taking the life of a human being. A baby will die. To the pro-choice ladies in the front row, I could see they were considering throttling me for killing that horse. Their compassion for the animal came through on their faces. The image of God was revealed in their love for horses. In contrast, their sinful nature came through in their adamant desire to make abortion of human babies the law of the land. This mindset is contrary to God's view of human life. To kill humans without issue and be horrified at the death of animals is a graphic demonstration of how sin perverts our image-bearing nature. Lest we be too hard on these ladies, we need to remember how much we struggle with ethics. We struggle because we desire freedom from the restraint of morality. If we let the Bible speak to us and develop in us its view of life, then we will find ourselves struggling with physical desires that are being restrained by the bible's moral law. Every one of us fails from time to time in these matters. That is why it is essential we have some standard calling us back to sanity and restraint. The Bible is an amazing document that gives us a basis for making these difficult moral decisions.

Should we reject the Bible as our basis for making moral and ethical decisions, there exists a dangerous endpoint: the inconvenience of morality sets up a slippery slope that devalues human life to the point that a society can believe they are doing right by eliminating inconvenient people like babies, various ethnic groups, and the infirmed. These issues are debated in America all the time. We are already on the slope. Between the years 1995 and 2011, American women "terminated" Down syndrome children via abortion at a rate of 67 percent (Natoli, 2012). Other articles note that Iceland has virtually "eliminated" Down syndrome babies by nearly a 100 percent abortion rate upon diagnosis[xxxviii].

Do not think for a second that it does not matter what you believe about where humanity came from. It matters greatly! If you get this wrong, it may cost you your life or the life of someone you love, or *could have loved*. If you believe that human life is a simple product of chance out of some primordial ooze billions of years ago, then the ethics of protecting human life has little basis. In fact, animal life may well be protected at the expense of human life in this new ethical camp.

In stark contrast, the biblical view states that human life is of great value. It is one of the ten commandments of Exodus chapter 20:13 "You shall not murder." The value of image bearers is stated in Genesis 9:5–6 which is I like to call *the Mandate of Human Government*:

> Genesis 9:5–6 (NIV84)
>
> 5   And for your lifeblood I will surely demand an accounting. I will demand an accounting from every animal. And from each man, too, I will demand an accounting for the life of his fellow man.
> 6   "Whoever sheds the blood of man, by man shall his blood be shed; for in the image of God has God made man.

This text is demanding an accounting in a community for the murder of one of its citizens. This text gives moral obligation and authority to communities and nations to develop a police force to investigate and punish murder. The basis of this mandate is that human beings are image bearers of God. This makes human life extremely valuable.

If you believe that human life was specially created by the God of the Universe and endowed with His image, you will develop a set of ethics that not only protects human life but also demands response when human life is taken either by an animal or another human being.

There are also dark days that come upon human life in which we despair of living. In those dark moments, we may even consider jumping from a bridge or putting a gun to our head. I want to remind all the readers of this book *that in those dark moments* that are common to humanity, remember <u>**you are an image bearer of the living God.**</u> *You are* *so valuable that after sin came into the world, the Creator Himself stepped into time and space and take the punishment of your sin. You are valuable enough for Him to die in your place.* If you're that valuable, you dare not take your own life. And remember this: the sun will come up again and shine on your face another day. When there is breath, there is always hope for tomorrow! Whenever things are troubling you to the point of ending it all, remember there are beautiful days coming. Trust your life, trust the days of your life to the Creator. Life is a gift, even the days of struggle. Do not listen to dark voices when thoughts of suicide penetrate your mind. Shout out to the darkness, "I will not end my life! I am an Image Bearer of the Living God! My life is valuable!"

Application to real life:

Q: Why is my life, your life protected by law?

A: We are image bearers of the Living God. This fact defines human life to be specially created. Each day of your life is of great value and is a gift from God

Q: Does that mean animal life is not to be protected?

A: Animal life is of value as well. It is just not on the level of human life. For an example of this, look at Jonah 4:10–11. Here the prophet was more concerned about himself and a plant than he was about the human life in the city of his enemies (Nineveh). Note that the Lord also includes the cattle that would be harmed if God judged the city. God has a concern for animal lives as well.

FOUNDATION EIGHT

Women: who can understand them?
Men: what happened to their brains?

Men and women…
The genders: why are we so different?

Society has imposed pressures on the genders causing
most of the tensions between the genders
OR
We were created to be different from each other

EIGHT

THE OTHER GENDER: WHY ARE THEY SO ... DIFFERENT?

Genesis 1:27
So God created man in his own image, in the image of God he created him; male and female he created them.

Where did the genders come from?

How is it possible that the reproductive systems of both genders evolved? It would have to happen independently. Without getting graphic, it is astonishing how precisely made are women for men and men for women. The evolutionary paradigm would have us to believe that over millions of years small changes brought about major effects in the lives of creatures.

Here's the problem:

In order for sexual reproduction to begin, both the male and the female must be fully functional in respect to reproductive capabilities. *Think about that for a minute.* The evolution of the male and the female must occur simultaneously and must occur completely in that first generation. Leaving aside the understood basics of male and female anatomy and the amazing design for each other, there are all the issues of timing for sexual reproduction to be successful. The hormone cycle of the female brings about a behavior change of reproductive receptibility. To enhance the potential of success, females produce pheromones that are sensed but not consciously perceived by the males, bringing about a strong attraction and increased interest in sex.

Further: the timing of sex is critical. The ovulated egg from the female has a very limited timeframe (12–24 hours) for it to be fertilized. The male sperm has a longer viability of up to five days. Timing of sex for the purpose of reproduction is vital for the survival of the specie. Everything must be in place, timed right, and body health sufficiently strong to allow implantation of the fertilized egg (zygote) into the prepared uterine wall. All of this timing in the body of the female is to prepare her for the male. In my wildest imagination, I can't envision a scenario in which the genders would evolve separately and become fully functional at the same time.

This is a serious problem for evolution. Statements like the following are typical of the vast array of article dealing with this subject, "More than 99 percent of multicellular ... [organisms] reproduce sexually and have *evolved elaborate ways to do so* [emphasis mine], including behavioral, physiological, and biochemical adaptations. So[,] there must be some enduring benefit. But despite years of observing, theorizing, and experimenting, researchers have been unable to pin down exactly what that might be. "Why sex evolved is very hard to answer," says Timothy James, who studies sex in fungi at the University of Michigan in Ann Arbor. "[Many] evolutionary biologists are trying to understand why it's so rarely lost, even though it's so costly."[xxxix] That is the catch. Sexual reproduction should never have evolved. It costs too much. It involves too many precise chemical and physical bodily functions in two separate creatures of the same species. It should never have evolved!

What makes the genders so amazing is that during the reproduction process, half of the genetic material from the mother and half from the father are joined together to make the child. This is a marvelous system of bringing diversity within the species. (Note for later: this is an amazing fulfillment of the marriage in which "the two become one flesh.") This is obviously a marvelously designed scheme. It is the father's sperm that will decide the gender. Each sperm is either male (containing the "Y" chromosome) or female (containing the "X" chromosome). Upon fertilization of the female egg by a sperm, the gender of the person is decided and directed by the "X" or "Y" of the fertilizing sperm. It is then that gender development can begin. The most interesting event to happen next is the newly understood development of different brain thinking patterns. Literally, certain parts of male brains are larger than female and vice versa. We actually develop our gender-specific brain thinking patterns while still in our mothers.

Development of the Distinct Male Brain

Many moms will testify that baby boys act differently from baby girls. It seems that their brains are already male by the time they are born. Some would even say, "Boys come out boys and girls come out girls (in behavior.)" We now understand that it is true. Boys have brain wiring different from girls.

The distinct development of the gender of a person's brain begins in his or her mother's uterus eight weeks after conception. Because both males and females contain an X chromosome, the growing human embryo begins with an undifferentiated female brain structure. It is only when the male Y chromosome (which is from the father and only in the male children) begins to exert its information on the embryo that the child begins to develop male thinking characteristics. The male Y-chromosome is the smallest of the human chromosomes and contains much less information than the X chromosome. It evidently takes a relatively small amount of information (two dozen genes) to differentiate the person into the male gender. Every cell in a person's body matches their gender. If you are male, every cell in your body is male; if you're female, every cell in your body is female.

Early in the development of the male child the testes develop, which will begin to secrete the male hormones, making major differences in the development of the person. It is interesting to note that near the turn of the twenty-first-century, we have come to understand that it is the secretion of the male hormones somewhere around eight weeks of gestation that greatly changes the brain of the child; it masculinizes the brain. (Sandra J. Kelley, 1999)[xl]

I know that many women suspect that men are brain-damaged and I'm here to say that there is some truth in what women have observed. One example is that of language skills. Women use both sides of their brain in the operation of language. Men tend to use just one side. This means that some of the connections between the left and right side of the brain are severed or fail to develop in the males. We are somewhat brain-damaged in that sense.

In the 1960s, when the feminist movement was gaining a lot of traction in our culture, there were a lot of people saying that males and females are no different other than physical anatomy. The idea was that we need to free women from the home, because they are just as smart and capable as men if given the chance (and in a very real sense this is true.) They also believed, and here is the error, that males and females behave differently *only* because of the molds forced upon them by their culture. If we change the culture, we will find there is no difference between the way men and women think.

Since that time, we have come to discover that is not true at all. Anybody who has raised children can testify quickly that little boys tend to come out rough-and-tumble and little girls tend to come out much gentler but verbally superior.

One early study would be useful to make a simple point (Williams, 1991). This study, utilizing mazes, was performed on rats. At the end of the maze was a rat treat. The researchers observed the animals solving the maze and then recorded the differences in how male rats solved the maze in comparison to female rats. They discovered that males were much more *driven* to solve the problem and find a solution to the maze whereas the females were more inclined to hang around in the center of the maze gathering with other females. What made this even more interesting was that the researchers removed the testicles on another group of male rats while the animals were still in the uterus of the female. This was performed before the male hormone had any effect on brain development. Now, being a veterinary surgeon, I stand amazed that they were able to do this. Nonetheless, they succeeded and now they had neutered male rats that failed to undergo the hormonal surge that masculinized their brains. When these surgically-altered male rats grew to maturity, they were turned into the maze. What the researchers discovered is that they tended to hang around in the center with the females. They were much less driven to "solve the maze." The removal of the male hormone in the uterus kept these male rats thinking like female rats. Their brains failed to masculinize.[xli]

What can we learn from this study? First: this research makes it clear that males do not think the same way as females, even in rats! This is not a huge revelation to most of us. Second: the cause is, at least in part, the testosterone surge early in the development of the animal or person. Kelley's article cited above suggests that female brains have increased communication of brain cells due to the influence of the female hormones. This may explain why men tend to be able to separate emotions from logic at an increased rate. This study also noted that the female hormones have strong menstrual cycle effects upon neurosensitivity, resulting in increased anxiety at specific times in the cycle. Most married men have come to readily recognize this effect. No fancy study was needed!

Not only is every cell in your body specific to your gender but so is your brain function and behavior. It is as though we were designed for different roles and functions in society and family.

With that scientific introduction to the origin of the sexes and our created differences, let me put on the pastor's hat and discuss the genders from the biblical counselor's chair. Without trying to come across sexist, there are things that tend to be universal in marriages and families. Understand that there will always be exceptions, and my observations come from a male perspective. Please allow me to indulge. In doing so, I may help a few relationships.

Those of us who have been married for a time and especially those who have children of both genders will certainly have observed firsthand many of these differences between male thinking and female thinking. I can tell you that the girls in my life are much more emotionally controlled than the boys. There are times when I can't figure out what the issue is other than there seems to be a lot of emotion in the female regions of the room. It is at times like these that us men want to try and fix the situation. We want to protect our ladies. This is an instinct of the human male. We want to solve the problem. We want to help. If there is a problem ... well, just leave it to us! We fix things. It is here that many of us men discover ourselves helpless in our quest. All of our great solutions are shot down in a flood of tears. As we listen to the issues at hand, our logic kicks in and we see the solution. Oh! This is simple. I can fix this! But when we offer our brilliant solution to the emotion and tears that are flooding the room, we soon discover that a logical solution was not what the woman was seeking! This is a perplexing part of being a husband. There seems to be a part of communication with our best friend that we simply are unqualified to address.

In a lot of these cases I have discovered that women have a lot of balled up emotion that just needs to get out. And so they verbally unload all that is pent up within them. Many studies, like Kelly's cited above, note that women are far better verbal communicators than men because women have enlarged communication centers in their brains. When there is a verbal barrage unloading, other women instinctively understand this and seem to know that it time to simply listen followed by a big hug. Many of us men are oblivious. I feel like the worst of these. A foolish man, speaking from experience, walks into the middle of such a situation thinking he can solve it with some logical answer when the real solution is to simply listen, comfort her, and let her unload.

Wakeup call for men: I can write all about this ... but when the events like described above take place in real time with my wife or daughter, I am absolutely compelled to try to fix the situation rather than just listen and comfort.... As I said earlier, men do have a certain level of brain damage.

Men, on the other hand, seem to have a fairly significant separation between our emotions and our logic. This is real handy when you need to provide food for the family requiring you to shoot a beautiful wild animal. The male logic overtakes the beauty of the animal, and he can pull the trigger with joy. He knows he has conquered the starvation factor and is providing for his family. Not only that, but this gives him bragging rights among other men. (Okay, this is my Montana - Dakota upbringing. In other cultures, it may be sports or some other form of conquering.) However, this separation of our emotions from our logic can have a terrible impact upon the man's relationships with the female gender.

In the human male, this separation between our emotions and logic appears to be a very real behavior characteristic. Our brains undergo dramatic transformation due to the testosterone surge in utero as described above. This results in distinctive anatomical changes in at least two different regions of the brain resulting in male behavior patterns.

I have observed in my own life that there are times when there's an emotion welling up in me and I cannot find words to deal with it. I just get frustrated and can't hardly speak. I usually must go away where it's quiet and just think. Some people give this character trait of human males a name: "going to the man cave." It seems like the emotional side of our brains short-circuits. We can't really get a hold of it and figure it out. Unlike females who have greatly increased verbal skills, many men find themselves struggling for an emotional outlet. If you want logic, that's available 24/7. If you want problem-solving, I'm the man. But if you want me to talk about how I feel… well, I don't really know how to do that. Sometimes I cannot even grasp what it is that I am feeling. When I say men are brain-damaged, of course I'm speaking tongue-in-cheek. Yet there seems to exist a real disconnect between the logic and emotions in a man's brain.

This characteristic of male thinking often frustrates women. Since they are in constant connection with their emotions and have great verbal skill, they just can't figure out why men have such an inability to share

their feelings. The answer is quite simple: the reason men don't talk about their emotions is that they have no clue what their emotions are. (Okay, maybe overstated… but consider the point). To men, emotions are those things we keep in control. We don't talk about them. If a man lets his emotions get out of control, it can be quite dangerous. I mean that in all sincerity. One reason a man will walk away from a verbal fight with a woman is as his emotions are welling up, he is in danger of losing control. Without the well-developed verbal outlet, our brains reach saturation. Often the only response a man has when his emotions are welling up is physical rather than verbal, so many men walk away to the "man cave" to let the emotions settle down. This is like pausing and letting the oil pour through the funnel when nearing the brim. It is unwise to push an argument with a man who is struggling with his emotions because there exists the ever-present danger that our emotional ineptitude will frustrate us to the point of actions we will regret. So, the wise man walks away when frustrated. The wise woman lets him go and cool down.

God made us different in more aspects than what meets the eye. We think quite differently, men and women. I suppose that is why we are so attracted to the other. We see things in the other person's character that draws us to him or her. However, living together with these differences is bound to bring about some sparks.

The Bible, being inspired by the Designer, provides us information about the different genders and God's intended differences in roles. What follows is a "hot potato" section of Scripture. It's a hot potato because it defines roles of men and women quite differently. The context of First Timothy chapter 2 is relative to church life and the roles of men and women:

> 1 Timothy 2:8–15 (NIV84)
> 8 I want men everywhere to lift up holy hands in prayer, without anger or disputing.

I know for many men in Western culture, lifting up your hands in prayer would be rather awkward. In the Jewish-Hebrew mindset, the men often pray standing up. They also raise their hands to the Lord in a gesture as if they were communicating to somebody just above them. Paul's point to Timothy points to male leadership in prayer in the family and church. Men are to be spiritual leaders in the home by design.

An important point here is that men are to do this without anger or disputing. Leaders must learn restraint and the ability to hear other points of view without digressing into an argument. Like I said earlier, little boys tend to come out rough-and-tumble. As they grow into men, they are the ones who more likely go hunting and play contact sports like football and rugby. This is not to say that women cannot be hunters and football players ... but when a group of men get together they tend to talk sports, hunting, motorsports, and the like. I have yet to personally find large groups of women deeply excited about such issues, although there are exceptions for sure. It is this nature of men to be involved and even excited in physically confrontational activities that makes the biblical warning against anger and disputing so practical.

Next, look at what Paul says about women in the church:

> 9   I also want women to dress modestly, with decency and propriety, not with braided hair or gold or pearls or expensive clothes, 10 but with good deeds, appropriate for women who profess to worship God.

Why is it that Paul addresses men about anger and disputing, but he doesn't say a thing about how men dress? However, he addresses women's apparel, and he states that women are to dress modestly, with decency and propriety. Their clothing is carefully defined as what would be appropriate for women who profess to worship God.

Women quickly learn that if they dress immodestly they will get a lot of attention from men. What many young women do not know about immodest apparel is that men are not at all interested in them personally, but only in what they see in the body of the woman. If a woman truly understood what runs through a man's mind when he sees her scantily dressed, she would be running for a coat, even if it's 90° outside! Men are visually attracted to the female body with sex in mind. The sexual sections of a man's brain are much larger than the female counterpart. Therefore, God warns women to dress appropriately because the effect on men is not what most women interpret when they get all the attention. Since God is the author of the masculine brain, He knows that exposure to improperly dressed women causes a lot of sexual stress. The male mind goes immediately to the act of sex when he sees too much of the female body. In the case of the man who wishes to remain pure in his relationships with women, this is troubling, whereas to the man who does not care to remain pure, exposed skin inflames his lust and he is more than okay with that. There even exists an element of danger to a woman dressing immodestly. Ladies, hear the scriptures and watch how you dress: if not for your own sake, then do it for the sake of the men in your life!

But there is more, and it is sometimes difficult for women to hear:

> [11] A woman should learn in quietness and full submission. [12] I do not permit a woman to teach or to have authority over a man; she must be silent.

For the twenty-first-century woman, this may be seen as one of those out-of-date ideas of the ancient Bible that has no place in human society any further. Please bear with me as I look closely at what is intended in these verses.

The Greek word for "woman" could correctly be translated as "a wife" based upon context. Let me show you how that would look (Pastor Kevin's Translation):

> [11] A wife should learn in quietness and full submission. [12] I do not permit a wife to teach or to have authority over her husband; she must be silent.

This is a legitimate translation, and it clears up a lot of issues. Paul's point is related to the roles in the family. The husband is designated to be the head of the household. This is not to mean he is the tyrant of the home. Rather someone must lead, and God has designed the men to have the neuropathways that are best suited for the final authority. We will see below that Genesis has God creating the woman as the helper for the man, meaning that she is right there alongside him. But when a final decision must be made, the man carries the weight of responsibility for what the family does. Therefore, in God's design for the family, the wife is not to have the final authority over her husband.

The text also states that she is not to teach her husband. The context here is teaching in a church where wife has the final say in regard to doctrine and Bible interpretation over her husband; this would be undermining his authority. There is an implication here that the brains of men are designed to make the tough critical decisions. This has nothing to do with intelligence. It is written to make clear that there are design differences that work best in certain roles. If this greatly bothers you, remember this: you are a product of a culture that has been steeped in an evolutionary agenda that does not recognize created design. In such a culture, you have every right to anything. *Nothing is defined by intention.* Everything is random and chaotic. The Bible, in contrast, states clearly that there exists a Creator. He created this world. He designed the male and female minds in human beings. You have a created intention! Discovery of your design and submitting yourself to the role that you are designed for will be the best for your life.

This is not to say that a wife cannot teach her husband anything; only a foolish man would not listen to the counsel of his wife. The point here is authority. In God's design, men are to have authority in their family. If you just stand back and look at how God designed the minds and bodies of men and women, it becomes evident that men were designed for the roles demanding strength. All men need to learn to grow in their leadership. All women need to learn to grow in their nurturing helping roles.

The rationale behind this order of submission and authority is found in two events in Genesis:

> 1 Timothy 2:13
>
> For Adam was formed first, then Eve.

The first point is the created order. That comes from chapter 2 of Genesis and is important to interject here:

> Genesis 2:4b, 7 (NIV84)
>
> When the LORD God made the earth and the heavens...⁷ the LORD God formed the man from the dust of the ground and breathed into his nostrils the breath of life, and the man became a living being.

First a little digression here about Genesis:

If you're reading this text for the first time, you might be wondering how this section in chapter 2 relates to what you just read from chapter 1. Chapter 1 is written in chronological order. Most of chapter 2 is written as a *parenthetical insert*. Look at this sequence of numbers below. Notice that the numbers are sequential. Then notice what is found in the inner parentheses:

$$1, 2, 3, 4, 5, 6 \text{ (details about 5 and 6)}, 7, 8$$

Notice that the chronology of numbers is interrupted by the words inside the parenthesis. When an author chooses to interrupt a sequence, he does so because he needs to stop the sequence and give information that does not fit neatly in the sequence; this parenthetical information is needed to understand what happened in the sequence. The author will continue the chronology following the parenthetical insertion.

Now let's apply this to Genesis: chapter one gives us the events in order as they happened in time. Chapter two then digresses and gives us information that is important for us to understand about the chronology. A parenthesis is *not written with an emphasis on time*. Rather it is written to make specific points about the particular events that took place inside the sequence. In this case, chapter 2 is telling us details about God's tender care in the creation of human beings. The creation sequence would be bogged down with all the details, so a good author often inserts the details outside the sequence so that we can first visualize the sequence without the clutter. Then the details are revisited in a parenthesis; in this case, the parenthesis is most of Chapter 2. The chart below gives you a visual illustration of how these chapters fit together:

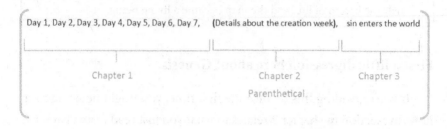

Notice very carefully that God made the man (we know him as Adam) before He made the woman (we know her as Eve). As I thought about this over the years, I realized that God could easily have made Eve first. He simply chose, out of His great wisdom, to make Adam first. After He made Adam, God showed him around the garden and pointed out the tree in the center of the garden from which he was not to eat the fruit. He could have waited until Eve was made and showed this tree to them both; we must assume there was intentionality on the part of God in making this first command to humankind in this manner. The first and most important doctrinal command to human beings was to not eat the fruit from this tree. Adam will be held accountable even though he will not be the first to partake of that fruit. His leadership role makes him the "fall guy." The buck stops with Adam, even though Eve was the first to take the fruit. Leadership carries with it intrinsic responsibility.

Now let's consider the creation of the woman:

Genesis 2:18–24 (NIV84)

[18] The LORD God said, "It is not good for the man to be alone. I will make a helper suitable for him."

First, I believe it is important to note the word "LORD" in this text. Notice that this word is given *all capital letters*. The translators have chosen to give you a clue to the identity of the Hebrew word used here that we translate into "LORD." This Hebrew word is the *name of God*. Sometimes you will see it written by a transliteration of the Hebrew letters: YHWH, or you may be familiar with it in another form: Yahweh or Jehovah. This is the covenant name of God. Those who are familiar with the 10 Commandments might be familiar with the fact that we are not to take *the name of the Lord* our God in vain. The name of the Lord our God is YHWH.

I am not exactly certain how to pronounce this name, but I suspect that "Yahweh" is reasonably close. In one of my seminary classes, a visiting Hebrew scholar spoke about this name. He believed that the name of God originates from the Aramaic verb "to be." If that is the case, then the name of God means that He is "the One Who is." This immediately reminds me of Moses standing before the burning bush asking God what his name was. God responded by saying, "I am who I am." Exodus 3:14 He is the self-existing One.

Now, let's apply this new knowledge of the name of God and what it means to our text in Genesis chapter two. "The One Who Is," "the I Am," spoke and said, "It is not good for the man to be alone...." The fact that it was the great "I am" Who spoke makes it extremely authoritative when He said that is not good for man to be alone. This man needed a helper. Better yet, this man needed a suitable helper; that is, he needed someone who is suitable for him.

Notice carefully what follows...it seems rather strange and out of place:

> 19 Now the LORD God had formed out of the ground all the beasts of the field and all the birds of the air. He brought them to the man to see what he would name them; and whatever the man called each living creature, that was its name.
>
> 20 So the man gave names to all the livestock, the birds of the air and all the beasts of the field.

Right here is where a lot of people have difficulty with Genesis chapter 2 in comparison to chapter 1. It seems to be out of order. Remember, this is parenthetical. He is giving us details that are important for us to understand relative to the events that occurred within the chronology of chapter one. He is telling us that the animals have been created and now God showcases them to the man so that he may give them names. A person has to stop here and wonder a little bit ... *why did God showcase the animals after he just said he was going to make a helper for the man?* I can imagine that it took considerable amount time (a few hours) to bring all the various types of animals before Adam and have him begin naming them. Everything from shrews to giraffes was paraded before him and he named them.

Stop for a minute: notice how this story is told. This is a technique often used in the Bible for the set purpose of building suspense. Here's what I mean: you should be asking these questions: Where's the woman? Where's the helper? We are drawn into the story and asked to see what God is doing to Adam. Look at what follows:

> ^{20b} But for Adam no suitable helper was found.

Do you see what God was doing? God was showing Adam all the wonderful animals and *each of them had their mates.* Adam now began to understand that **none of these were specifically made for him**. He was being prepared to see something magnificent:

> ²¹ So the LORD God caused the man to fall into a deep sleep; and while he was sleeping, he took one of the man's ribs and closed up the place with flesh.

Observe here the very first surgical anesthesia. It was performed by God on the first man named Adam. The purpose of the surgery was to remove a portion of the man's side. Did you notice I did not say "ribs?"

This is a rather unfortunate translation. The Hebrew word here is not limited by definition to just "ribs." The Hebrew word speaks of his "side." This is a crucial detail for us to understand the role of men and women correctly. God is making it abundantly clear that even though Adam was made first, the woman was made from *his side*. She was not made from his foot, so that she would be under his foot (that she was lower than him). Nor was she made from his head so that she would be over him (superior to him). Rather she was made from the side, as an equal, a companion. And to make this point even more abundantly clear, I want to remind you of how God spoke of creating mankind in chapter 1:

Genesis 1: 27 (NIV84)

27   So God created man in his own image, in the image of God he created him; male and female he created them.

Both male and female human beings were created in the image of God. There exists no distinction **in value** between the male and female genders in the Bible. There does not exist any distinction **in superiority** between the genders. We just see a distinction in **roles in the family**.

Now let's continue with the text from Genesis chapter 2:

---

22   Then the LORD God made a woman from the rib he had taken out of the man, and he brought her to the man.

God brings her to him. Adam first lays eyes on this woman named Eve. The words that burst out of his mouth are recorded in Hebrew poetry ... the beauty of which is missed in the translation to English:

---

23   The man said, "This is now bone of my bones and flesh of my flesh; she shall be called 'woman,' for she was taken out of man."

In the Hebrew writing style, we have intensification in the poetry.

When he says bone of my bones and flesh of my flesh, the writer is increasing the intensity of the words in the poetry. I have heard it translated this: WOW! This one is from me and she is for me! WOW! We will call her woman, which means "out of man." This was a moment of ecstasy. He had been looking at shrews and lions and giraffes, and now he's presented a beautiful woman and she's a magnificent gift to him (as he is to her). That is why the text concludes this topic with these words:

> [24] For this reason a man will leave his father and mother and be united to his wife, and they will become one flesh.

What does this last statement mean? It is because of the attraction between the man and the woman that they will separate from their parents and be united together as one (a new family unit). The word that we translate "united" could be translated "glued." When a man leaves his father and mother and is joined with his wife, the two are glued together. In the process, they become one body. In God's amazing design of the genders, he intended for the male and female to be such close friends that they act in an almost choreographed unison as they progress through life.

Over the years, I've observed older couples. It is interesting to eavesdrop on their conversations. Many have their own communication system developed through the years of difficulties and joys. Let's eavesdrop in on one such hypothetical conversation: "You know, dear, it's been a lot of years since we've taken an excursion south...." Before the other one can finish the sentence, the response comes: "I know you're right; I miss them as well." This is a code that none of the rest of us can break. We have not put in the years and gone through the trials that afforded this couple such closeness of thought.

> There exists no distinction *in value* between the male and female genders in the Bible ... we just see a distinction in *roles in the family.*

Oneness like this is purchased through time—time together. This is part of what's intended when the text speaks of them becoming one flesh. Their time together results in a depth of understanding of the other person that accepts the flaws and strengths of the other. No longer is there a need to change him or her. He loves her as she is. She loves him even knowing his routine failures.

Just a note here: many couples quit their marriages too soon. They face a time of struggle (as all *brain-damaged-men* do when they marry *emotional-verbal-women*).... We all are flawed. This struggle is quite predictable in my counseling experience. (Between three to seven years of marriage will bring a time of difficulty in most marriages). By quitting now, they have not had the time needed to really understand their *one-flesh* counterpart. They have only noticed that the person they married is not the person they imagined they married. Reality has set in. *I married a flawed person. I do not like some of the flaws I see. I am embarrassed by some of the flaws ... I can't live with these flaws!*

With the divorce behind them, they search for another who will meet their needs. Alas, they find themselves starting over again in the process of trying to learn another person. Often that fails as well and never do they live together long enough to develop the one-flesh relationship that most people desire. *A good marriage is not just the result of finding the right person*, though that is important. A good marriage takes time and dedicated effort in learning the other person, loving them for who they are, flaws included. In the end is it worth the journey because deep down inside everyone wants to be loved for who they are ... yes, flaws and all.

Incredibly, there is another part that we dare not miss. The product of the sexual intercourse of the couple is a child who is half the genetic code from his mother and half from his father. The child is truly "one flesh" of the parents. God's design for life is incredible!

We are not complete with our work in 1 Timothy, Chapter 2. There is more to observe ... and it gets sticky:

> 1 Timothy 2:14–15 (NIV84)
>
> And Adam was not the one deceived; it was the woman who was deceived and became a sinner.[15] But women will be saved through childbearing—if they continue in faith, love and holiness with propriety.

The man was given authority in his household because he was created first. But there is another reason. Adam was not deceived into eating the forbidden fruit of the tree. Eve was. (This is an event to be discussed shortly when we reach Genesis Chapter 3.) The text seems to imply that Adam was not deceived: Eve was. Some conclude that men have ability to see through deception better than women. I do not believe that this is necessarily true. Many times my wife, by virtue of her female wiring, is able to make me aware of deceptions. I have concluded that the issue here is she was deceived and that will result in sin and death in the world.

What, then, does this text mean when it says, "the woman will be saved through childbearing?" The text is implying that the woman will find her greatest peace and joy in life in the roles that surround raising a family. This does not exclude her from other roles in community and business, but her heart will generally find its greatest joy in the nurturing role in family life.

How do I come to such conclusions?

The word we translate "childbearing" is likely a synecdoche[xlii] which is a figure of speech where a part represents the whole. Let me give you an example of a synecdoche so you may envision how this figure of speech may be in play here. Think of two young men standing on a street corner on a warm summer evening. A fancy hot rod blasts by and one young man shouts out, "Wow, take a look at that set of wheels!" Was his interest limited to the wheels? No, in this case he was using the wheels to represent the entire car. Applying this to our text, we see the likelihood that Paul is using childbearing to represent the entire role of women in family and church as the nurturers. This would reflect their created design and family role.

What about the single woman?

Certainly, marriage is not guaranteed. Nor is marriage ever simple or easy. For some, marriage is not in the picture, at least presently. If this is you, consider this: the role of nurturer is something beautiful to emulate in a woman's life. To the unmarried woman, I give this application: find ways to be that person who excels in helping others do well. This may be in your church, community, and/or workplace.

How does this relate to the woman being saved? Salvation in the Bible carries multiple ideas that progress through the life of people. Let me give you three definitions of salvation followed by points of application to help you understand the differences:

1. Salvation from the consequences of sin

    a. Believing in Jesus' death on the cross to pay for our sin and keep us from God's righteous and just punishment
    b. Belief in Jesus moves us from an eternal destiny separated from God to one of in the very presence of God. (Hell to heaven)

2. Salvation from the sin character in our lives

    a. Growth to maturity as a believer in Jesus
    b. Sometimes called sanctification, this is the process of becoming more like *Image Bearers of God* throughout our life on earth. (More about that in chapter 10.) This is the process of literally becoming holy. This process is never complete in this life. We are constantly moving toward holiness or away from holiness as we submit (or not) to the teachings of God's Word.

3. Salvation from the very presence of sin

    a. This occurs in the final eternal state of people when God destroys this universe by fire and recreates a new one where the very memory of sin and death are removed.

The salvation found in childbirth is referring to the second one, salvation from our former sin character. The context confirms this when the text adds:

---

1 Timothy 2:15b (NIV84)

...if they continue in faith, love and holiness with propriety.

So, salvation found in childbirth speaks to the growth of women toward maturity as believers in Jesus as they assume their created roles as godly women. This may also allude back to another role that women hold that men cannot. It will be through the female gender that the Messiah will come, the One who will save her and all of mankind. More on this will be forthcoming in later chapters.

Now let's stop and put this together in application to our lives. The American culture is moving very rapidly toward a feministic view in which the distinction of the genders is blurred. The feminist movement is not to be completely dismissed in that it is very important that our culture honor the female gender as a completely equal human being. The movement has exposed some of the many abuses of men who dominated the Western culture. But the movement has also attempted to minimize and even erase the clear created differences between men and women. This is destructive in many ways. At the very least, feminism sets up competition between the genders and in the more extreme cases it demonizes men so that we feel that being masculine is something we need to be ashamed of.

The Bible gives us a different view. Since biblical Christians recognize that God is the Creator and Designer of life, we understand that He intentionally designed differences in the genders including our brain designs. That being the case, it is in the best interest of all humanity to discover their gender and celebrate the way they were created.

Celebrate your gender and learn to excel your role as a man or woman. Work with your God-created design rather than working against it. Learn how to function with your limitations and your spouse's limitations. Men: celebrate your wife's femininity. Women: celebrate your man as the strong partner he is.

Application to real life:

- Men and women are equally created as image bearers of God, being totally equal in value.
- The woman was created with flesh taken from <u>the side</u> of the man being totally equal in relationship. Neither is superior to the other.
- The man was created first. Therefore, God designed him for the role of leadership in the family.
- The woman was created to be a helper to the man. This means that her role will be more submissive, yet alongside her man.
- The thinking processes (brain wiring) of male and female human beings differ greatly. God created our minds for the role He designed us to play in the family, church, and community.
- When people join in marriage they are glued together. This is not designed to be separated without great pain and loss. We divorce each other at great peril to our physical, emotional, and spiritual health. This great damage extends to the children, the "one flesh" of the marital relationship.
- When people put years into their marital relationship, a spiritual "one flesh" relationship develops. This is what men and women, deep down inside, desire from human companionship … but

only those who persevere through the trials, arguments, and difficulties of the early marriage will experience it.

Since the Bible was written through the inspiration of the One Who created the genders, a person has two choices:

- You can rebel against the role God has given you in your gender.
- You can embrace the role God has given you in your gender

I recommend the latter.

FOUNDATION NINE

How can evil exist in a world created by a good God?

Is He not powerful enough?

NINE

YOU SAY A *LOVING* GOD MADE THIS WORLD?

Elie Wiesel

Elie Wiesel grew up as a child of the Talmud (Jewish tradition and commentary on the Old Testament of the Bible) in his little Transylvanian village of Sighet. He came to love the evening discussions he had with Moshe the Beadle, a foreign Jew residing in his village because of his deep heart for God. Moshe the Beadle also had a Rabbi-like fondness for Elie and his tender heart for God. Then one day the foreign Jews, which included Moshe the Beadle, were rounded up by the Hungarian police. He would have died with the rest of the trainload of Jews except for a miracle. He was shot in the leg and fell into the mass burial pit with the thousands of others. He remained lifeless for terrifying hours until he could escape into the darkness. This was followed by months of harrowing flight and a will to survive in order to return Sighet to warn everyone. Upon his arrival, his impossible story was met with total disbelief. No one acted. No one left. In 1944, Hungary was taken over by the fascists who sold out their Jewish neighbors to the Nazis. Eventually the entire village of Sighet was captured and deported to the extermination camps, but not before Moshe the Beadle fled late in the night.

In his book, *Night*, Elie describes the sheer terrors that he experienced at the hands of the Nazis. The book is much more than a historical account: it is the basis for his philosophical rejection of the Jewish God of his heritage. What is the reason for Elie's rejection of God? Listen to his own words as he describes his father's loss of faith which will be soon his:

> Never shall I forget that night, the first night in camp,
> which has turned my life into one long night,
> seven times cursed and seven times sealed.
> Never shall I forget that smoke.
> Never shall I forget the little faces of the children,
> whose bodies I saw turned into wreaths of smoke
> beneath a silent blue sky.
> Never shall I forget those flames which consumed my faith forever.
> Never shall I forget that nocturnal silence which deprived me,
> for all eternity, of the desire to live.
> Never shall I forget those moments which murdered my God and my
> soul and turned my dreams to dust.
> Never shall I forget these things, even if I am condemned to live
> as long as God Himself. Never.[xliii]

Elie's emersion into the deepest bowels of human depravity stole his faith in God.

C.S. Lewis

In the days following the death of C. S. Lewis' wife, this grief-stricken man went into a depression during which he questioned everything he'd come to know about God. In his book *Through the Shadowlands*, Brian Sibley chronicles the response of Lewis to his deep and desperate grief when faced with the death of his beloved wife, Joy. Brian says this about Lewis,

"People expected Jack [his nickname] to find consolation in his faith, but he couldn't, 'Talk to me about the truth of religion and I'll listen gladly. Talk to me about the duty of religion and I'll listen submissively. But don't talk to me about the consolation of religion or I shall suspect that you don't understand.'

"Time and again he constructed complex arguments of faith only to find them demolished by his grief as if they were no more than a house of cards... Jack had arrived, more by anguish than by logic, at an extraordinary theory: supposing God were bad?"

Lewis himself had this to say after considering his loss and after reading the works of Elie Wiesel:

When the capability of absolute evil within humanity is witnessed along with God's apparent silence in response, one has to wonder if God exists or if He's simply indifferent to the suffering of people.[xliv] C.S. Lewis

It is here, when all the evil and horrors that occur daily on this planet are considered, that the atheist cries out from their own painful past and poses this question to the Christian and the theologian, "How can your all-powerful loving God, Christian, create a world like this, a world full of suffering, pain, murder, and death?"

Just a cursory look at this world demands that the Christian thinker take serious the atheist's question. Why is this world so painful? And when you're standing over the lifeless body of a dearly loved one, even the most devout must conclude that something is wrong in this world. In those times, everyone struggles with how God could allow this beautiful person to just disappear from existence on this planet.

Kevin Horton

I am very hesitant to share my personal story. I rarely can get through it without great emotion from the scars, but it is applicable to today's lesson:

I remember the day very well. It was a clear spring day, May 16, 1990. I squeezed one more cow into an already hectic spring schedule. I stepped out of the veterinary hospital and enjoyed the clean mountain air and

A cattle head catch is pictured here. The animal is pressed through the corral and its head is captured by closing the gates.

the bright sunshine reflection off the snow-crowned peaks to the west. It would be the last morning for five long years in which I would enjoy anything, let alone hold a clear thought. The horror of those days are a haunting remembrance deep within me.

My 10:30 AM appointment was to examine Brownie-the-cow. She had not been eating for a few days. The animal had been recently moved to rented pasture upon the mountainside. She was not at her owner's ranch where there existed quality animal handling facilities. When I arrived, she was held in an old rundown corral that had suffered the deterioration of too many spring rains and winter snows. It did have a somewhat functional cattle chute and head catch. Since this was likely a stomach issue, I chose to use the head catch rather than roping her. I would likely have to pass a stomach tube through her mouth; a rope around her neck would impede that. The rancher and I pressed Brownie into the chute and captured her in the head catch.

I completed my examination and treatment when I noticed that she had developed some lacerations on her right rear leg from fighting the treatment. I leaned over to look at the cut leg when the gate latch broke. I failed to notice that she had her powerful left rear leg pushing against the gate. The gate functioned like a crossbow at full draw. The failure of the latch functioned as the trigger. Unfortunately, my head was next to the gate. I was in the crossbow. I was the arrow. The gate impacted my head and catapulted me through the air across the coral to the railings 30 feet away. That moment proved to be life-changing for Dr. Horton and his family. Never would it be the same.... Never.

After many tests at the capable hands of physicians and a battery of psychological exams to determine the extent of the injuries, my neurologist named my condition *post-traumatic syndrome*. Syndromes are a group of disorders of unknown or unexplained causes that they lump into one place and give them a name (something-something Syndrome). From my perspective, this syndrome was a never-ending migraine that would narcoleptically induce me into deep sleep 16 hours a day. I could hold coherent thoughts for moments, but they were only moments. On one of those early visits with the neurologist, I was informed that the next two years would be diagnostic to the rest of my life. He went on to say that after two years, whatever condition my life was in is what I should expect it to be like for the rest of my life. That was rather ominous to say the least.

Now, backing up to the day *after* the injury: I tried to resume my veterinary duties. My veterinary technician was forced to take me by the hand and remove me from the exam room because my mind was stuck like an old LP record caught in a grove. I was unable to speak; I just kept repeating a hand motion but no words came out of my mouth. I had no idea. I have since come to learn that people with neurologic disease are oblivious to the extent in which they've been harmed and the symptoms they present. I remember examining a cat in the days that followed. I gave the owners seven very logical steps that I would take in diagnosing the animal's problems. I could remember great detail about things that took place before May 16, 1990, including all my veterinary training, but my short-term memory was nonexistent. On that day when I walked 10 feet out of the exam room to my pharmacy,

> How can your all-powerful loving God, Christian, create a world like this, a world full of suffering, pain, murder, and death?'

everything went blank. I could not remember any one of the steps I had just told them we would do; I could not even remember the symptoms that the animal was presenting. I now knew I was in trouble.

Over the following weeks and through trial and error, I learned that by taking caffeine in high doses, I would have enough conscious time to perform minor surgery, after which I would be passed out in the dark in my office while frantic secretaries tried to reschedule appointments. I learned to live with constant pain. It never stopped; it just intensified and subsided in waves. The pain and delirium resulted in a dramatically changed personality. I was prone to rage and I rarely smiled.

During one of the routine neurology appointments, I recall the doctor explained to my wife, Cori, and to me that 70 percent of the marriages that involve a spouse with a head injury of this severity will end in divorce within five years. During those days, and in one particular case following one of my now routine outbursts, I clearly remember Cori gathering the children together around her like a hen gathers her chicks under her wings. My three young sons were weeping and fearful of what would happen between their mom and dad. Cori said to them, "Boys, divorce is not an option in this family." Cori knew well the expectations of marriage laid out in the Bible, and she bravely held to her vows.

I lived the following months-leading-to-years in nightmarish fog. I have not retained much of the details in my memory of those horrific days, but there is one day I will never forget. It was another routine trip to my neurologist. I intended to discuss with him the fact that none of the medications he had prescribed really had much lasting effect. In reply he said these words to me, "Well, Kevin, it's been two years…." My memory was severely damaged, but I remembered crisply the two-year timeframe that whatever is the state of my medical condition, it will be permanent. I gasped. My mind raced (as much as my damaged brain could) and thought, *This is what my life will be like from now on? Will I never again be able to remember what happened 5 minutes earlier? Will I remain prone to these outbursts of anger and then retreat to sleeping hours upon hours?*

Will there be no end to the pain until death? How could you allow this to be, God?

The neurologist continued by explaining that there was one more drug he could try. The problem with this drug is that it is an older drug with a specifically terrible side effect. A small percentage of the people who take this drug chronically developed severe heart disorders that lead to death. In order to prevent that from happening, a person must withdraw from it for two weeks twice a year. Time would prove that those two weeks were as close to hell as I ever could imagine. You see, the drug worked quite well. I still slept maybe 16 hours a day but my time awake was much closer to normal. I was less prone to outbursts and most significantly, the pain was close to tolerable. I began to develop a livable pace of life and the family was adjusting to the "damaged but livable dad."

Inevitably, the day would come when I had to face the two weeks in hell—they called a *drug holiday*—where I stopped taking the medicine cold turkey and the drug was slowly being metabolically removed out of my body during the first two days. Then came hell. I would be rolling around on the floor of my home in agony. We would darken the room to reduce the neurological stimulation. Cori would sympathetically rub my back for hours, trying to relieve the pain. The kids learned to cower. They were not to make any noise; it could cause me to uncork. The *drug holidays* became sheer terror to me. I simply cannot explain to you what it was like in the weeks of anticipation leading up to the next scheduled "holiday" and then the hellish two weeks until the day I could begin to take the medicine once again.

> Time would prove that those two weeks were as close to hell as I ever could imagine.

But things were going to get worse, much worse.

December 12, 1994, four and one-half years after the accident, Cori left the church service in the middle of my sermon.... There is one more detail I must tell you ... of which I now cringe at the timing. In the middle of all of the turmoil in our lives, I had become a bivocational pastor of a church plant in the northern portion of my veterinary practice. This was not the time for me to become a pastor—no way! Yet in my delirium, I foolishly applied for that position. I look back at that decision and just shake my head. Somebody with a head injury of that extent should not be in church leadership. But that is where I found myself.

On that Sunday after the service was over, I found my lovely thirty-nine-year-old wife lying on the floor of the church entrance in agonizing pain. I would be six weeks before we would understand what happened. Her heart attack was missed by two separate hospital emergency rooms. Finally, weeks later, the diagnosis was made: we were informed that most of the left side of her heart was dead from the heart attack that took place six weeks previous. Her heart was sufficiently beating from the edges just to keep her alive. Her life expectancy was just days to a maximum of two years; she remained on earth for a total of five months after we heard the doctor's diagnosis.

On a pristine May afternoon I was lying in my hammock, enjoying the sun. This was the hammock the boys had recently given me. Suddenly, my oldest son came running frantically outside and told me that Mom wanted to "see me." I admit I was reluctant to get up and leave this moment of basking in the spring sunshine. My son corrected his communication with words that penetrated me deeply, "It's the heart thing, Dad!" I now noticed his face, which completed the story. I was stirred to immediate action. Bursting into the home, I found my wife in cardiac arrest. She was purple and in a tremor. I massaged her heart and gave her artificial respiration. After about 30 seconds of CPR, she revived for a moment. Her eyes came back to center and then locked on to my eyes one last time as she said, "Kevin, I love you." Then she was gone. I would hold on to her last words for months to come. To this day, the cries of my youngest son penetrate my memories with his anguished cries, "Mommy! Mommy!" A few hours later we were standing in the emergency room. Our oldest son touched her lifeless, bloated, purple body and sobbed out of sheer panic, "Dad she's so cold. Why is she so cold?" How can a mentally damaged father protect and nurture his children in such days?

The Horton family had come to understand suffering, and we were now introduced to grief.

I did not understand grief before, nor could I have. Until you are there, you will never understand how deep and dark it is. Could things get darker than this? I did not think so ... but I was wrong.

I was scheduled for a drug holiday a couple of weeks after Cori's death. I skipped it. But the clock kept ticking and another six months passed. I was now forced to undergo the hellish drug holiday. This time, however, I had to go it alone. I do not even know where my sons were during those two weeks. I imagine I had made arrangements for them. I simply remember that I was all alone rolling in agony on my living room floor day after day, night after endless night. I was as alone as a man can possibly be ... alone in my agony. It was then I cried out in great anguish, "God, I do not think I can take much more of this. You promised in the Bible that you would not give us a temptation beyond what we could handle. This trial: alone, in sheer agony, and widowed with three desperately struggling sons, is beyond anything I can handle. God, make me better or take me out; take me home to heaven."

> During days of terror: this world does not look like it was created by a good God

I'm sure my sons could give you another perspective. Their perspective would be of a world in which they were very secure before May 1990, after which everything in their young lives crashed down all around them. Everything that they knew for certain was shaken.

Even though human tragedy happens every day and we hear about it on the radio or read about it in the newspaper, it is a whole different thing to walk through it personally. It is during those dark days of the human experience that people discover that this world can be a disastrous place. During such days, it does not seem to reflect the love and goodness of the Judeo-Christian God. It does not look like a world created by a **Good God**.

And so, the atheist joins the unison of suffering, exclaiming, "Why would your loving all-powerful God, Christian, create a world like this one, full of suffering, pain, grief, and death?" *And it is upon those dark days that their words take hold.*

This is one of the most fundamental and crucial questions that must be addressed and answered if any Christian theology is to be found to be reality. We must ask the question boldly and seriously right along with the atheist... Why, God, did you create a world like this? Why do people die? Why is there such great suffering in this world? I thought when you finish creating this world you declared it to be very good. What happened?

And we forget our sin.

We forget our responsibility.

This question must be answered. We must let the Bible speak to the human situation and why this world is like it is.

How We Got Here:

We left off our study in Genesis with the man leaving his father and mother and being joined with his wife and the two becoming one flesh. What follows is a most peculiar verse. It kind of hangs out there as if it were misplaced and no one knew where to put it so someone just stuck it on the end of chapter 2:

Genesis 2:25 (NIV84)

25 The man and his wife were both naked, and they felt no shame.

The man and his wife were both naked and they felt no shame.... Okay, what's the point? It is vitally important in your study of the Bible that you notice these hanging verses. Since God inspired this text, then this hanging verse has a purpose that should be revealed somewhere further in the text. We will find that to be true, in this case, as we delve into chapter three … into the Garden of Eden. For the moment, just let that dangling verse be. We will return.

The Serpent's Story

Let's now look at the famous story of the Garden of Eden and the forbidden fruit:

> Genesis 3:1 (NIV84)
>
> 3   Now the serpent was more crafty than any of the wild animals the Lord God had made. He said to the woman, "Did God really say, 'You must not eat from any tree in the garden'?"

This text begins with a rather sticky problem. We now have an animal, a wild animal that is particularly *craftier* than the other animals. Furthermore, he speaks. He speaks to the woman and she speaks back as if this were normal.

In the process of considering this text carefully, I noted that the word "serpent" is fronted. If you recall, fronting means that the noun is in front of the verb. It is my observation that fronting in Genesis introduces a new topic. The topic for the next fifteen verses is "the serpent." Therefore, we need to define very carefully who the serpent is. Genesis 3:1 helps a bit in that it tells us plainly that the serpent is one of the "beasts of the field." Recall that the Bible has a sort of taxonomic classification of land animals relative to how they relate to humanity. The "beasts of the field" are larger animals (as compared to the creeping animals) and are generally not fit for domestication. In Genesis 1:25 they were called "beasts of the earth." This difference is likely an expansion of the description of the animals

The Hebrew word for "serpent" [נָחָשׁ "Na-chash"] is generally translated as a snake. That translation is based upon the word usage after these events when the animal, the beast of the field, is cursed. More on

that in chapter 10. This word has some usage where it represents a dragon.
[xlv] This reminds me of a reference in Revelation chapter twelve. Here is
recorded an incredible story about a great dragon in heaven. Verse nine
says this about the dragon:

> Revelation 12:9 (NIV84)
>
> [9] The great dragon was hurled down—that ancient serpent called the devil,
> or Satan, who leads the whole world astray. He was hurled to the earth,
> and his angels with him.

This serpent-dragon in this apocalyptic story is actually Satan, one of
the fallen angels who leads a rebellion among the angels against God. These
angels end up being what we now call demons. Some of you may have difficulty in believing in the devil and demons because you were taught that
it's myth. But the Bible makes it clear that Satan is very real. He is a very
real spiritual being. Furthermore, the Bible states that there exists a large
number of other angels who fell into rebellion against God with Satan.
They are created creatures who, like us, have the ability to decide right and
wrong. This group made the foolish decision to rebel against God. They
did this before the rebellion of humanity. The book of Ezekiel[xlvi See Ezekiel 28:15]
in the Bible tells us that sin originated from within Satan.

Throughout the non-Western world, many people practice local ver-
sions of animism which is the belief that various plants, animals, and even
rocks have spiritual power that, in most cases, must be appeased. People
who practice animism have had real-life experiences with spiritual forces
(demons) that control their lives. They know that they must sacrifice to
them and heed their demands or their lives will be tormented. Even when
they do heed and offer sacrifices as demanded, these creatures torment
them relentlessly. The world of fallen angels (demons) to many people in
the Eastern world is well understood ... and greatly feared.[xlvii]

The serpent[xlviii] in the story of Adam and Eve is the fallen angel named
Satan. Why, then, does the text call him a wild animal? The only answer

that makes sense in this case is that Satan had come to indwell the animal that was called a serpent. We know that demons can indwell animals, as demonstrated in the Gospels when Jesus allowed a legion of demons to leave a man and indwell the pigs on the mountainside. ^{Matthew 8:28–34} Therefore, in our text, the serpent must be a wild animal that was indwelt by the fallen angel Satan.

The next significant player in this drama is the One who was called the LORD God. Notice, once again, that the word LORD is written in all capital letters signifying that it is a translation of the covenant name of God, YHWH.

The final player in the early part of this drama is the woman, the wife of Adam named Eve. She is evidentially alone at the time that the serpent approaches her. We aren't told how long it has been since she was created, but we do know that everything in the world around her is new. Unlike a newborn babe whose mental capacities are just beginning to kick in, this woman's brain was at full function the day she was created, and on this particular day she hears an animal speak to her. To us, this would be a monumental moment: we would be off to the circus to make our millions. Contrastingly, Eve is experiencing life with a mature mind, though totally ignorant of what life "should be like." In this new world before her, she discovers that this serpent-dragon talks. This is just one more new discovery in this amazing world that God has created. The language ability of the animal is most likely a manifestation of the power of the fallen angel Satan. He is using the animal for his dark intentions.

Let's see what Satan has to say to the woman:

Genesis 3:1b (NIV84)

He said to the woman, "Did God really say, 'You must not eat from <u>any</u> tree in the garden'?" (Emphasis mine)

Right here it is important to remind ourselves of what God *actually* said about the trees and their fruit. In Genesis chapter 2 God said this to Adam:

Genesis 2:15–17 (NIV84)

[15] The LORD God took the man and put him in the Garden of Eden to work it and take care of it. [16] And the LORD God commanded the man, "You are free to eat from any tree in the garden; [17] but you must not eat from the tree of the knowledge of good and evil, for when you eat of it you will surely die."

Notice that Satan's words are deliberately in error. From this section, we can develop a few thoughts about how Satan does tempt us.

The first principle of temptation is that the woman was alone. Satan will often work on us the most when we're isolated from other people. This is particularly true of Christians who are isolated from the rest of the Christians in the world. Jesus instituted the church as a place where Christians can join with one another to mutually grow in the faith. God has also given us the church as a place of safety. It is when we're in fellowship with other believers that we have the most protection. It is important to remember that the church is not a building. The church is a gathering of other people who believe in Jesus. *We are in most danger of temptation when we are alone and isolated.*

The second principle that we can identify is *that Satan will deceitfully twist the words of God for his own purposes.* One interesting concept to be aware of in the interpretation of Hebrew story (narrative) literature is that it uses a high amount of imbedded speech. The first words recorded by a new character are almost always important in giving us a picture of that person's character. In Satan's first words, he deliberately twists God's words to deceive people.

Watch what happens when Satan made this deliberate lie to the woman:

> Genesis 3:2–3 (NIV84)
>
> 2 The woman said to the serpent, "We may eat fruit from the trees in the garden, 3 but God did say, 'You must not eat fruit from the tree that is in the middle of the garden, and you must not touch it, or you will die.'"

The woman was forced to respond to the error of the serpent. She defends God by stating that they could, in fact, eat from any of the trees except, of course, the tree in the middle the garden. Yet she goes on and *adds to the words of God*. She says that they're not only disallowed from eating the fruit, but they are not to touch it. Eve is making God out to be stricter than He is. Did Adam add this directive to his bride as a protection? We cannot be sure. But the woman has made God out as stricter than He actually is. She ends her statement by correctly stating that if they do eat from this fruit they will die.

The serpent immediately moves in. He has hooked her into his temptation by forcing her to respond to his misrepresentation of God's command. She demonstrates that she is ripe for temptation when she responds by making God strict. This strict God now appears to not be looking out for what is best for Eve. He is **restricting them** from even touching this fruit; Satan is ready to set the hook like a skilled fisherman:

> Genesis 3:4–5 (NIV84)
>
> 4 "You will not surely die," the serpent said to the woman. 5 "For God knows that when you eat of it your eyes will be opened, and you will be like God, knowing good and evil."

The hook is set with the most blatant lie, "You shall not die." He follows the lie with an explanation as to why God would lie. According to Satan, God is not looking out for what is best for her. He is holding back his best from her. If she will just listen, she will understand that if she eats this fruit she will be like God. She will know good and evil.

Satan's last statement is partly true. *Notice that the best lies contain a large percentage of truth.*

The hook has been set and now it's just a matter of the person thinking about what Satan has said ... *Maybe God is not so good after all. Maybe He is holding back from us. Maybe that fruit is the key to us becoming like God himself. Maybe, Maybe....*

Once the hook is set, the spiritual fight begins. What follows is a very real example of how temptation works on the human mind. Once we allow the thought that God may not be so good and that He is not looking out for our best, we are now set to explore the world of rebellion against God's ways (sin) and see endless possibilities.

The text appears to allow some time to pass as the false ideas of Satan begin to work in her thoughts. I wonder how many times she passed that tree and contemplated its fruit. Finally, the fateful day comes and Adam is with her:

Genesis 3:6 (NIV84)

6 When the woman saw that the fruit of the tree was good for food and pleasing to the eye, and also desirable for gaining wisdom, she took some and ate it. She also gave some to her husband, who was with her, and he ate it.

There are three basic temptations that still haunt humanity today:

1. Good for food. This is something that is good for our bodies and satisfies our cravings.
2. Pleasing to the eye. This is something that is beautiful and we desire it for our own.
3. Desirable to gain wisdom. Finally, this is something that will make us wiser than the rest of humanity.

NOTE: These are not evil within themselves. It is the context in which we satisfy our desires that makes something evil. For instance, for the woman to see a fruit and desire to eat it to satisfy her cravings is not wrong. In this case, the context tells us that this particular fruit is forbidden. So, it is the context of something forbidden that these temptations function.

If I look at all the things that entice me, it seems like every one of them fits into one of the three categories (see 1 John 2:16). The three basic temptations of Eve are the same temptations that we experience today.

The sad news is that Eve fell for the lies of Satan; after examining the food and seeing all the potential benefits that God was holding back from her, she ate some. The most astonishing part is that Adam was now with her, and he also ate.

Application to real life:

Are there temptations that haunt you? Are there desires in life to which you are strongly vulnerable to being tempted? Understand that these temptations haunt everyone. If you are struggling with a sin issue, you can be sure that 30 percent of the people you pass by each day are dealing with the same problem. What makes me so certain? Your sin susceptibility is simply a version of the same list that enticed the woman:

There are three basic temptations that still haunt humanity today:

1. Good for food. This is something that is good for our bodies and satisfies our cravings.
2. Pleasing to the eye. This is something that is beautiful and we desire it for our own.
3. Desirable to gain wisdom. Finally, this is something that will make us wiser than the rest of humanity.

Everyone is facing the problem of sin. That is what the church is here for. To help each other gain freedom from the sin that so wants to take us down. Eve failed when she was alone. Protect yourself! Get involved in your local Bible-teaching church and find a group that can help you grow in the faith toward maturity.

FOUNDATION TEN

Curse and Restoration

TEN

You Have Been Cursed!

We have yet to explain clearly why this world, which is sometimes beautiful and then, in a moment, turns to darkness and absolute despair, is like it is. We have yet to satisfactorily respond to the atheist's objection. Do you remember his question? How can your all-powerful and loving God, Christian, create a world like this one ... full of pain, suffering, grief, and death? If we respond that it is simply the result of sin, we have not given much of an answer. As we enter this chapter, we will begin to see how the world, which was originally very good, dramatically changed into the world that we were born into, a world full of suffering, pain, grief, and death.

Up to this point in Genesis chapter 3, the man and the woman have been functioning completely on their own. God now enters the scene and searches out for His rebellious creatures. But first Adam and Eve[xlix] must begin to feel the effects of their sin.

Genesis 3:7 (NIV84)

7   Then the eyes of both of them were opened, and they realized they were naked; so they sewed fig leaves together and made coverings for themselves.

Recall that strange, seemingly out-of-place, verse from the end of Chapter two:

Genesis 2:25 (NIV84)

25 The man and his wife were both naked, and they felt no shame.

Before sin entered the world, they were naked and without shame. In other words, they could look upon their own body as well as their partner's body and see nothing wrong with them, nothing to cause their faces to turn red. Since sin entered the world, shame immediately entered their lives. They could not look at each other and themselves without passing judgment. Suddenly they realized they desperately needed to cover their shame. People experience shame when they realize that they fall short of expectations. Adam and Eve have discovered themselves to have fallen short of what is expected of beings that bear the Image of God. What was previously marvelously good is now seen through the lenses of judgmentalism. Adam and Eve responded by covering their shame with clothing made from plant material.

Our sin always finds us out

Genesis 3:8–9 (NIV84)

8 Then the man and his wife heard the sound of the LORD God as he was walking in the garden in the cool of the day, and they hid from the LORD God among the trees of the garden. 9 But the LORD God called to the man, "Where are you?"

Maybe a day passes. Maybe it was later that evening. The two humans certainly had enough time to sew together their fig leaves. In the evening[1] God was walking in the cool of the day in the garden that He planted for the man. The way this text is written, it sounds like this was a normal routine for God to be walking in the garden in the early morning or evening to meet with Adam and Eve in a loving relationship. Evidentially, God appeared in the form of a man. Many theologians, including myself, believe that this is what we call a theophany: an example of the appearance of the Lord Jesus Christ on the Earth in human form before the incarnation, before His birth in Bethlehem. There are a few other times in Genesis where we can observe these theophanies. In later chapters of Genesis, you can observe the *Angel of the Lord* appear to the patriarchs. See Gen 16:7–13, 22:10–17 In those stories this Angel will do things that only God can do, yet is in the appearance of a man. Those events are theophanies as well.

By the way these verses tell this story, we can surmise that when God appeared in the garden before they sinned, the man and the woman came running. But on this day things are awkwardly different; they hear God and hide. On this day, they go the other direction.

Here's a foundational principle: sin separates us from fellowship with God. The sin of Adam and Eve separated them from the close fellowship they had with God their Creator ... the sweet fellowship that they experienced just maybe hours earlier.

What we have described in this change in relationship with God is tantamount to *spiritual death*. Death means separation. Adam and Eve died spiritually. Their relationship with God exists in separation. They now feared God ... and they had good reason to fear Him.

What happened next is of utmost importance:

God sought out the rebels, the sinners. There is no doubt that he knew what happened. He knew where they were hiding. It is really quite silly to hide from God ... but people do it all the time. Maybe at this reading you find yourself hiding from God. Maybe you are running like the biblical prophet Jonah. Maybe you have the same reactive response typical of human behavior since Adam and Eve. We run and hide from God. Some even pretend that He does not exist. This deeply broken relationship is the result of our failures and sin. We are ashamed and we hide or we defame the name of God to make ourselves feel less dirty.

> Genesis 3:10–11 (NIV84)
> 10 He [Adam] answered, "I heard you in the garden, and I was afraid because I was naked; so I hid."
> 11 And he said, "Who told you that you were naked? Have you eaten from the tree that I commanded you not to eat from?"

Right here we uncover an important principle. I wish I could get it in my head. I wish I could get it so well understood in my brain that it would change the way I act when I am tempted. It is a truth that is the same today as it was in Adam's day. What is this life-changing principle? It is this: our sin will always find us out. Adam responded to God and explained why he had hidden. He was naked. Little did he know that by admitting he was experiencing shame because of his nakedness, he was admitting that he had eaten from the forbidden fruit. His sin found him out. It always does. We may get away with it for now, but there always is that final accounting with God. Our sin will always find us out!

Passing the Buck

Now confronted with the reality that they have broken God's commandment, Adam must answer God. Notice what sinners do when they are put on the spot. Maybe you will see yourself here. I see me:

> Genesis 3:12 (NIV84)
> 12 The man said, "The woman you put here with me—she gave me some fruit from the tree, and I ate it."

When sinners are confronted with their sin, they routinely pass the buck. Strangely, Adam expertly performs this. It's like he has had years of practice. He first blames the woman...you know...the very same woman that he shouted out with great exclamation when he first saw her, the woman whom he said was bone-of-his-bone and flesh-of-his-flesh ... this woman had, unfortunately (in Adams mind and statement to God), turned out to be a terrible mistake ... (Notice how Adam made her into a convenient excuse).

Not only is the woman blamed here, but so is God, as Adam recounts in his statement, "the woman _you_ put here with me." Interpretation: God, you really made a mistake sending her to me! (That is gutsy, Adam; rebuking God! I don't suspect that will work out too well for him.)

God seems to ignore the rebuke. He ignores Adam's blame-game for the moment as He lets the people dig their own graves (so to speak) and turns to the woman:

Genesis 3:13 (NIV84)

13 Then the LORD God said to the woman, "What is this you have done?"
The woman said, "The serpent deceived me, and I ate."

Following in her husband's footsteps, the woman deflects her guilt and blames the serpent. No one wants to take responsibility for their sin. As the great King Solomon says in Ecclesiastes, "There really is nothing new under the sun." We do this all the time.

The Curse:

Why is the world like this?

Why is there suffering and death?

It is time to explain why this world is like it is. The following verses are crucial in discovering how God's original creation changed.

As we enter this next section, which breaks out into Hebrew poetry, observe two different characters enveloped in one name. In verse 14 of Genesis 3, the Lord is speaking directly to the animal that was called the serpent. In verse 15, he is addressing the demonic spirit that has taken control of that animal. A curse is about to be pronounced upon this animal. Originally, before this curse, the serpent-dragon was some sort of 'beast of the field' class of animals. That is about to change:

Genesis 3:14–15 (NIV84)

14 So the Lord God said to the serpent, "Because you have done this,

"Cursed are you above all the livestock

and all the wild animals!

You will crawl on your belly

and you will eat dust

all the days of your life.

The serpent is forced to crawl on his belly and eat dust all the days of his life. If the idea of eating dust is to be taken as a figure of speech, then we can conclude that this livestock animal was changed into what we know as the snake today. In other places in the Bible, to eat dust implies total defeat Micah 7:17, lam 3:29. It seems a bit strange that God would condemn the animal because he was misused by Satan. Shortly, we will see that the entire creation is cursed because humanity rebelled against God. How does God reason this? Is it because everything was placed under the authority/dominion of humanity? It is perplexing. I must leave that one to the wise counsel of God.

Verse 15 looks beyond the animal. In this verse, God is speaking directly to the demonic spirit, known as Satan, who indwelled the animal. This prophecy in Genesis is of utmost importance. Read it carefully:

---

5 And I will put enmity

between you and the woman,

and between your offspring and hers;

he will crush your head,

and you will strike his heel."

The prophecy speaks of strife between the woman and Satan. This text implies a future battle involving the offspring of the woman is looming. This child will crush the head of Satan. The picture given is of a strategic and final battle that leads to the destruction of Satan. But in the process, this offspring of the woman, this *Son of the Woman*, will be harmed by Satan. He will suffer a strike on the heel. Notice that the picture here is that of a snake biting the heel of a person and the person then smashing the head of the snake with his foot.

Most Christian expositors recognize this text as being the first prophecy of the coming Messiah or Christ. It is the first prophecy that will be fulfilled with the coming of Jesus. In this prophecy, it is the *Child of the Woman* Who will crush the head of Satan. There is something in this prophecy that is quite unusual. In Hebrew culture, children are always spoken of as the son of their father. Yet this prophecy speaks of a child who was *the Son of the Woman*. This does not make sense in and of itself until we reach the New Testament times and see that the baby Jesus was not conceived by a human father:

Luke 1:26–35 (NIV84)

26 In the sixth month, God sent the angel Gabriel to Nazareth, a town in Galilee, 27 to a virgin pledged to be married to a man named Joseph, a descendant of David. The virgin's name was Mary. 28 The angel went to her and said, "Greetings, you who are highly favored! The Lord is with you."

29 Mary was greatly troubled at his words and wondered what kind of greeting this might be. 30 But the angel said to her, "Do not be afraid, Mary, you have found favor with God. 31 You will be with child and give birth to a son, and you are to give him the name Jesus. 32 He will be great and will be called the Son of the Most High. The Lord God will give him the throne of his father David, 33 and he will reign over the house of Jacob forever; his kingdom will never end."

34 "How will this be," Mary asked the angel, "since I am a virgin?"

35 The angel answered, "The Holy Spirit will come upon you, and the power of the Most High will overshadow you. So the holy one to be born will be called the Son of God.

Marvel at this prophecy in Genesis; it was written at least 1400 years[li] before Jesus' day. This prophecy speaks of *the Son of the Woman* as the One who will crush the head of Satan. Remember, this prophecy does not speak in normal Hebrew terms. This Son is not named after his father because, in the case of Jesus, He was born without a human father. So, in this early prophecy, the Christ, the Messiah is named after his mother. This prophecy gives us a glimpse of the incarnation.

Who in their wildest dreams could ever have imagined such a tale? The commentators and codifiers of Jewish law over the centuries (such as the Mishnah and Talmud) never foresaw the virgin birth. A virgin conceiving was something nobody had even considered as a possible fulfillment of this text in Genesis. It is only in retrospect that we can see this prophetic mystery revealed. This is one of the most amazing prophecies in the Bible and it was literally fulfilled in the virgin birth. Jesus was literally the *Son of the Woman* and not a son of any human man.

Now consider the fact that the serpent will strike the heel of the child, *the Son of the Woman*. The serpent will inflict injury upon this child. An injury of this nature would be painful but not terminal; in a spiritual sense, this implies damage in battle but not ultimate victory. The prophecy also states that *the Son of the Woman* will crush the head of Satan, implying his ultimate demise. At the cross, Jesus was inflicted with great pain and died physically. By this great sacrifice, He destroyed the works of Satan, and eventually will judge Satan completely and send him to the lake of fire [Revelation 20:10]. The right to forgive mankind was purchased in that battle. Just ahead we will observe that this prophecy comes on the heels of the curse, the curse of death that will shortly be pronounced upon all humanity. Therefore, this prophecy is the first hint that God will turn things around and make the terrible news of sin and a cursed world into something none of us could have imagined. The cross is seen in the strike of the serpent to the heel of the *Son of the Woman*, by which forgiveness, available for all of mankind, was purchased.

It is because this story is totally unimaginable and the fact that it comes together over the course of thousands of years of prophetic history that makes it so compelling. Most every human being considers the big issues related to how we got here and where we go after death. I urge you to consider the supernatural nature of biblical prophecy and fulfillment in the person of Jesus Christ. This prophecy is the first of over 300 that will literally be fulfilled in Jesus' conception, birth, life, death, burial, resurrection, and ascension into heaven.[lii]

The Woman's Curse

God now turns from the serpent to the woman. The Hebrew word for "woman" is fronted indicating that the topic has now shifted from Satan to that of the woman.

> Genesis 3:16 (NIV84)
>
> 16 To the woman he said,
>
> "I will greatly increase your pains in childbearing;
>
> with pain you will give birth to children.
>
> Your desire will be for your husband,
>
> and he will rule over you."

With every child born I am increasingly thankful for my gender. I have observed and assisted in the process of giving birth by many domestic animal species. The stress and pain, swelling and tearing of sensitive tissue, and all that comes with the process seems like a huge price to pay on the part of the female gender for reproduction. I also was present at the birth of three of my sons. No one is going to tell me that this prophecy is not to be taken literally. There is, by my observation, an intense amount of pain and suffering associated with the birthing process. No, thank you: I will take the male gender that God has gifted me with!

Really, though, I must confess I am very thankful for mothers, for my mother, and the mothers of my children. (Yes, mothers, for I have children born from three different moms!ᴸⁱⁱⁱ) They went through a lot to bring us into this world. The curse has cost them a lot!

The second part of the prophecy has to do with the relationship between the male gender and the female gender. Since conception occurs as a result of the attraction of the male and female to each other, it seems correct, considering the context, to see that there's a change in that relationship. Before sin entered this world, the male and female relationship was considerably smoother. Any of us who have been married know that marriage is not simple. A good marriage takes a lot of work and a lot of pride-swallowing. The reason for this is because *these relationships are under the curse*: the woman will desire for her husband but he will rule over her.

The Hebrew word that we translate into "desire" is used in two different instances, beyond this text, in the Old Testament. The first case is regarding the children of Adam and Eve and is found in the next chapter of Genesis in the story of Cain and Abel. In this case, God has rejected Cain for the offering that he brought. He tells Cain to do what is right and warns him that if he doesn't, sin will control his destiny. God uses a figure of speech to make this clear to Cain. God personifies sin as if it were animal. He speaks of sin like a mountain lion crouched and ready to attack:

> Genesis 4:7 (NIV84)
>
> 7 If you do what is right, will you not be accepted? But if you do not do what is right, sin is crouching at your door; it desires to have you, but you must master it."

Sin has a *desire* to take control of Cain. We learn from this text that one meaning of the word for *desire* is for one to have "control over another."

The other usage of the word "desire" is in Song of Solomon Song of Solomon 7:10. In this case, the word *desire* is speaking of the husband's desire to have a physical relationship with his wife. These are the two other usages of this Hebrew word that we translate "desire" as found in the Bible.

Now let's apply this to our text. In the first case, which is found in the very next chapter, we see that the definition for the word *desire* has to do with an animal's *desire* to devour another. Since this is the meaning of the word chosen by Moses in the next chapter and the only other definition to be found was written by King Solomon some 500 years later, good Bible interpretation techniques choose, if the context allows, the definition used by the author to be his intended meaning. This helps us to be reasonably certain that this was Moses' intended meaning when he chose this Hebrew word. It would be quite reasonable, therefore, to say that what is implied here is that the woman will *desire* to have a devouring control over her husband, but he will have the final rule over her. In other words, by this curse, the battle of the sexes has begun. The woman will *want* control, but the man will *take* control. Neither response will result in a great marriage. This curse is why the apostle Paul was so adamant about a woman not taking authority over her husband. Women, according to this curse, will have a desire to take the role God designed men to have.

Some of you might be irritated by all this. I understand. After all, there is a history of men lording over women. In many places in the world, this results in terrible tyranny. The Bible is not speaking of tyrannical rule. It is speaking of final authority vested in the man because God designed the man's body (brain thinking patterns and physical strength) to be the leader of the family. Do not forget that in the created design the woman was not taken from under his foot. She was taken from his side. That ends the idea of tyranny. It is a mutually edifying relationship that respects both parties. But to reject the created design is to place a different form of tyranny into the relationship. This is the overreaction of our present culture that fails to recognize the difference between men and women. It then expands the overreaction by removing the final authority of the husband. In essence, this overreaction neuters the husband and weakens the family unit.

The Man's Curse

Now the curse moves to the man. Adam, the man is fronted. He is now the topic to be addressed:

Genesis 3:17–19 (NIV84)

17 To Adam he said, "Because you **listened to your wife** and ate from the tree about which I commanded you, 'You must not eat of it,'

Husbands, pay attention to the text. This is what happens when you listen to the voice of your wife!

Okay, okay... I was just kidding!

Adam was ultimately responsible for his actions and the actions of his household. It is one thing to enjoy the fact that men are given the authority over their households. It is a whole other thing to understand the responsibility that comes with that authority. Men will be held responsible for the decisions of their household. As a result of his failure in the management of his household, Adam receives a curse on his work. This curse now is passed down to all of mankind because the entire planet's ecological systems have been cursed. The world is now thrust into what Darwin observed and named *the survival of the fittest*. Plants and animals now struggle to find their place in this world. Those that do not find their place perish. Look at how God explains the tentacles of the curse that spread out over the entire planet:

"Cursed is the ground because of you;
 through painful toil you will eat of it
 all the days of your life.

Work, that was a joy of Eden, is now necessary for survival. Not only is it necessary but it is to be difficult. New words are added to the human vocabulary: "painful" and "toil." The words "days of your life" foreshadow an end to life. Life on the planet has just moved from "very good" to "toil until you die."

> 18 It will produce thorns and thistles for you,
>   and you will eat the plants of the field.
> 19 By the sweat of your brow
>   you will eat your food

Ecology is the study of plants and animals and their relationship to their environment. The entire field of study just came into existence on this day of history...and it came with a vengeance. Thorns and thistles...structures on plants that cause harm to animals are now coded in the DNA of plants. These plants will infiltrate gardens, forcing the keeper to pull them out. If left to themselves, these weeds will take over the newly tilled soil, crowding out the plants intended for food. Gardening takes work. Gardeners' backs hurt, fingers swell from the toxins in the thorns, and the sun beats down on them during the day. Thanks, Adam.

Mankind up to this point only ate plant life. All people were vegetarians. It is highly possible that all animal life was vegetarian at this point as well. A number of years back when studying the book of Isaiah, I discovered that the great lions will one day be able to eat straw. Straw is different from hay in that it is the dry yellow leftover plant stalks from harvesting seeds. Hay is made up of grasses cut while they are still green and is much more digestible. Cattle are able to eat coarse feeds like straw because they have a four-chambered stomach. The first two stomach chambers work like a fermentation vat in which the bacteria therein breakdown the coarse stalk material (fiber) and make it available for heat in the winter and releases some nutrients for absorption. A dog or cat cannot make any nutritional use of straw because they have the simplest stomach and intestinal anatomy. Digestion of meat protein requires the least complex digestive system. To be able to digest straw requires a very complex digestive system like that found in cattle and deer (they are cud chewers and have multiple stomachs—ruminants).

Look at what the text says in Isaiah:

Isaiah 65:25 (NIV84)

25   The wolf and the lamb will feed together,
      and the lion will eat straw like the ox,
      but dust will be the serpent's food.
      They will neither harm nor destroy
      on all my holy mountain,"
      says the LORD.

In this prophecy, the lion is pictured as an herbivore that is capable of digesting straw. A dramatic change in the digestive anatomy of the lion species will be required.

The context of this prophecy is in the future, apparently in either the Millennial Kingdom or the New Heavens and the New Earth:

The Millennial Kingdom is the 1000-year reign of Christ on this earth following the Tribulation Period spoken of in the book of Revelation [Rev 20:1-3]. The other possibility for fulfillment of this prophecy in Isaiah is the New Heavens and the New Earth [Rev 21, 22]. This is when the present world system will be burned by fire [2 Pet 3:7, 10]. I interpret this burning with fire to be understood that the entire mass of the universe will be converted to energy. Then God will recreate a new heavens and new earth that will be eternal. The present heaven and Earth cannot be eternal because all life requires energy from the sun. But over time the Sun will burn out. This is true of all the stars of the heavens. Eventually they will all burn out. Once again, we have one of those amazing moments in Scripture where we see a very scientific concept being taught to nonscientific people. Since the stars will burn out, God must recreate the world and energize it with light that comes from Him rather than energy that comes from the stars. This is the only way there can be an eternal New Heavens and New Earth.

There exists another purpose for this new creation of our eternal habitation: fossils and bones. In many parts of central Montana, as it is in many areas around the world, we find fossils. These are reminders of death and destruction. In the new heavens and new earth, God will wipe away the tears and memories of death and destruction. Look at the future guaranteed for all who believe in Jesus's work on the cross for the forgiveness of sin:

Revelation 21:1–4 (NIV84)

1 Then I saw a new heaven and a new earth, for the first heaven and the first earth had passed away, and there was no longer any sea.

2 I saw the Holy City, the new Jerusalem, coming down out of heaven from God, prepared as a bride beautifully dressed for her husband.

3 And I heard a loud voice from the throne saying, "Now the dwelling of God is with men, and he will live with them. They will be his people, and God himself will be with them and be their God.

4 He will wipe every tear from their eyes. There will be no more death or mourning or crying or pain, for the old order of things has passed away."

Notice the restored Eden here. God is with man again (vs. 3). The tears and suffering of this life is gone. By recreating new heavens, the dying source of light (stars, sun) are replaced with the light that comes from God Himself and will never dim. By recreating a new earth, He has removed the record of death and suffering from His people. No one will stumble on the bones of a deceased person or animal.

When this happens, there also will be animals on the new Earth. The wolf and the lamb will be feeding together, indicating that they are no longer in a predator-prey relationship. The wolf will be eating grass like the lamb. Not only that, but lions will eat straw like cattle. The lion will exhibit the anatomy of a ruminant (like a cow) and a wolf may be a pseudo-ruminant like a horse.

Here is the point: with the cross, we start to see a reversal of the curse that Adam brought upon this world. The Millennial Kingdom [Rev 20:1–3] will see dramatic reversals in human government (which has the function of restraining sin [Genesis 9:5–6].) Government will finally be free from corruption.

Government will function with the *Son of the Woman,* the Messiah, as the world's king. Sin will be restrained. Finally, in the New Heavens and the New Earth all the effects of sin will be reversed and removed.

Here's the process:

The Creation

- *Was* very good
- *Presently* is cursed
- *Will be* restored to a very good state.

Below I have developed a graph that depicts the fall of a very good world into a deeply cursed world. As the graph progresses, things eventually are restored to a state that is even better than very good. Why is it better? Because the people in the New Heavens and the New Earth cannot fall into sin ever again. We will have had that experience and have no longer any temptation to make that mistake again! We will finally receive the ultimate end of our salvation: the total removal of sin.

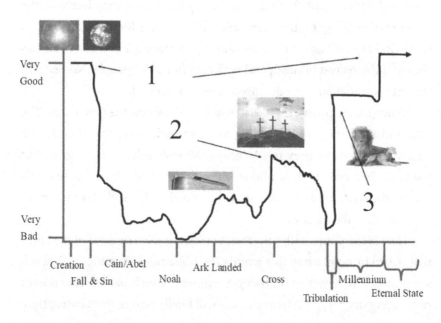

1) Notice how the world was very good in the beginning. It will be once again restored in *the New Heavens and the New Earth*. See Revelation 21-22

2) The Cross of Jesus is the point where restoration of the curse begins.

3) *The Millennial Kingdom* sees the greatest movement toward restoration with the Messiah reigning over the entire earth. See Revelation 20:1-10

Today, we live under the effects of the curse of sin. We witness murder, rape, theft, corruption, and more. This world is no longer "very good." There exist in our lives wonderful sunny days where its warm rays shine on the green farmland. There are also days in which God blesses us with rain on the crops. Such days remind us that there is a *Good God* Who created all of this.

But dark days also come. And one day the darkest day will arrive.

The curse to Adam is not complete:

> until you return to the ground,
> since from it you were taken;
> for dust you are
> and to dust you will return."

Life on planet Earth has now moved into the realm of vanity. A man will work hard all the days of his life, toiling at his work through sweat and great difficulties to finally get a little ahead … and then to die. We are returned to the dust, making our lives essentially meaningless. When a man finally gets enough to be secure, our bodies are worn out and we cannot enjoy the fruit of our labors. Eventually we return to the ground.

Is God Just Mad at Us?

Is God just mad at us? Is this curse simply a judgment upon us? Or is there a deeper and greater purpose in the vanity of life? Adam, his race of people and the entire creation, has been subject to death and suffering ^{Romans 8:19–24a}. When people experience the depths of this suffering, there exists a natural response toward God. Ellie Wiesel, C.S. Lewis, Kevin Horton, and many of you have experienced suffering in life firsthand. Some people turn toward cursing God. Some others end up questioning their faith. They do not understand how a good God could allow this to happen. Maybe you have asked that question. Maybe some of you have cursed God in your anger and grief. How does all of this suffering fit into Christian theology, Christian thinking? What is the answer?

Consider this: the curse follows directly after sin. The earth and all life on this planet are cursed. In the curse is the promise of the coming *Son of the Woman* Who we now know as Jesus, the Son of God. At His first coming, Jesus took on human flesh. He became 100 percent human (all the while still being 100 percent God). Because He was human, He took the effects of the curse up Himself. He took on the potential for hunger and thirst ... and He experienced those very cravings. He also took on the potential for suffering ... the suffering of death. God the Father placed His Son on this earth in a human body under the curse that humanity brought upon this world. He sent His Son with one main purpose in mind: to **die** on a cross for the sins of humanity so that all who believe in Him will be saved from the ultimate curse of *eternal* separation from God. He sent His Son to redeem the world of humans.

Here is the point we need to grasp: if humanity were not under the curse of death, then we would not be redeemable. Our condition would be like that of the angels who followed Satan. They do not die, thus they are unredeemable. The curse of death is, then, the only means that humanity could be forgiven for their sins. The curse of death has been turned into a blessing by the cross! I find myself marveling at how God

> The curse of death is, then, the only means that humanity could be forgiven for their sins. The curse of death has been turned into a blessing by the cross!

takes a curse and reverses everything. That is the Christian message. It is a message of hope in a world gone mad. It is a hope that God will reverse all the terror *our* sin has caused.

The restoration message is more than just a restored *heavens and earth*. The restoration message is about *people* who believe and how God is restoring the image of God in them, in you. Remember, when God created mankind He created us in His image. We were given attributes of God such as love and justice. But with sin now in us, all the sons and daughters of Adam and Eve exhibit the attributes of Satan as well. The purpose of the cross is to *restore the image of God* within us! When a person believes in Jesus' death on the cross to forgive their sins, the Holy Spirit of the Living God enters that person. As that believer submits to God in prayer, reading, and learning to understand the Bible, and fellowship with other believers, they grow in the faith. The end goal of our faith is full restoration to the image of God. We are being restored into the complete image of God to which we were intended. The death curse has brought us life through the death of the Son of God! Restoration into the full image of God, to the image to which we were intended, began at the cross and then individually when a person believes in Jesus.

The theology of the Cross is, then, directly related to the curse of death. Now, what this means is that when death was pronounced on this planet (when Adam sinned), there existed a view to the restoration of people. The restoration came when the *Son of the Woman* was born. The restoration was paid for with the death of the *Son of the Woman.*

Now let's return for a moment to the other views on how to interpret Genesis: in the other views, millions of years of death and suffering were in the design from the beginning. In these methods of interpretation, death is not a result of the curse but was in the original design. For

> The restoration message is more than just a restored heavens and earth. The restoration message is about people who believe and how God is restoring the image of God within them....

this planet to be declared "very good" by God and yet animals were designed to suffer excruciating deaths for millions of years would not make God to be very good.

Take this a step farther. All the fossils that are found in sedimentary rock around the world are evidence of animals that have died. If Christian theology is to be found to have any validity, then death had to begin with the curse that came in Genesis 3. All the fossils found throughout the world would have to originate *after* Adam. The origin of the vast majority of the fossil record would then have to be from the worldwide flood of Noah. To believe in millions of years of evolution before the curse of Adam would be to destroy the theology of the cross.

This is no minor issue. Either the Bible is correct on this or it is not. If it is not, find your peace somewhere else. In that case, the Bible would be a false book. However, if it is correct, then the clear majority of scientists, museums, and centers of higher education are wrong when they assert millions of years of evolution. Pure faith requires you to make a choice.

> "How can your all-powerful loving God, Christian, create a world like this, a world full of suffering, pain, murder, and death?"

Either way, it will be a decision of faith. Either you place your faith in the hands of men who are *studying the creation* or you place your faith in the hands of the God Who *made the creation*.

What, then, is the answer to the atheist's question?

If you mix evolution and millions-of-years-of-death into your theology, then the Bible has no answer. Death was in the original design. The fossil record makes this clear. The atheist question above remains unanswerable by the Christian world.

In contrast, when you allow the Bible to speak for itself, then we do have a solid answer:

- This world as we observe it is **not** the original created design.
- This world is *a cursed world* because of humanity's rebellion against God's good ways.
- We suffer directly from the sins of others as they commit crimes against us.
- We suffer disease because this is a world under the curse of death.
- Ultimately, we die as a direct result of our sin.

If the story ended here, it would only be an explanation without any resolve or hope. But it does not! ***God cursed this world with a view to the redemption of people.*** He cursed us with death in order that He may redeem us (pay the price for our rebellion) from the second death called hell. This redemption was purchased with death. The Son of God stepped into time and space and took on a human body that was subject to death. By His death, the curse is reversed. Ultimately, the goal of our redemption is the restoration of humanity to be clean and true image bearers of the Living God … as we were designed to be!

How do we answer people who have suffered?

What can we say to comfort Ellie Wiesel, C. S. Lewis, and all who have questioned God when they feel the fury of death and evil?

When we blame God, we forget our own sin. We forget that a portion of the evil of this world is because of the effect our own sin, my own sin, has had upon it. We somehow image that we ourselves are the good guys and those who harm us are the bad guys. We ignore the fact that our own sin has contributed to the hell of this world.

I remember well the day in 1999 when Columbine High School was under siege. This was the first of many days of terror upon our school campuses. Everyone was asking why. Why would someone kill their classmates? What kind of evil can cause such behavior?

In asking that question, we are isolating our own sin from the question. Here is what I mean: as the events that surrounded the Columbine Massacre came to light, it became clear that the perpetrators were seeking two groups of people to kill:

- The athletes
- The Christians

The reason they targeted the Christians gives evidence that they were under demonic influence. The reason they targeted the athletes was that they suffered greatly by those bullies all their school days.[liv] They were getting even. As I read articles about this event, it suddenly struck me that I can pass judgment upon those two boys and what they did. I would seem right to do so.

It was later that I connected my past behavior to the athletes at Columbine. A haunting memory of the look on a young man's face as I pressed him up against the lockers in my high school days flooded my mind. You see, I had been bullied most of my elementary and middle school days. But when I got to high school, I grew strong and became an athlete. In my sophomore year in high school, I reversed roles and began bullying a young man. I can see, to this day, the terror in his eyes as I had fun at his expense. Oh, how I regret that today.

Here is the point: I can judge the Columbine perpetrators easily enough ... but what if that young man, the one I pushed around, snapped one day. What if he came to school with a gun because of my sin? What if all the trauma I caused him led to his breakdown?

I now realize that *my sin* is part of the evil of this world. *Every time I*

194

sin, no matter how small it may seem to me, I add to the cumulative horror of life on planet Earth. Every time you sin, you are adding to the cumulative horror of life on planet Earth.

Response:

So how do we answer people who have faced great terror and witnessed death of their loved ones and then cry out against God? Well, of course we console. We offer great empathy and cry with them.

That we can do. But how do we answer the question … the question of "How could you let this happen, God?"

You have forgotten your sin. Your sin is part of the terror of this world. When I was injured by that cow in 1990 and my wife died in 1995, this was part of the ramifications of living in a world of sin … **of which I have contributed**. My sin, every small insignificant sin and every large and terrible sin, adds to the terror of this world. I am part of the problem. When a person blames God, they have forgotten that the sin of humanity is the issue. We have rejected God's ways and are now reaping the harvest.

> Every time I sin, no matter how small it may seem to me, I add to the cumulative horror of life on planet Earth

Remember this: God will redeem us from the terror one day; He will redeem those who believe in His Son. So when the dark days appear, remember redemption is coming! He has begun redemption in your life right now … from the moment you believed. He gave you the Holy Spirit Who is working in your life to bring about change in your behavior. The Holy Spirit is working to restore the image of God in you this very day! As you read your Bible and learn of its truths, you begin to change. God has begun the process of renewing you already. Further, there is a future that is even greater than anything we can imagine. The Millennium is coming! The

New Heavens and the New Earth are coming! If you are a believer in Jesus, then God will redeem you and finish restoring you to the image of God and He will place you in that magnificent new world....

It's just a matter of time.

POSTLUDE

WILL YOUR THEOLOGY ANSWER
THE QUESTION?

We have addressed C. S. Lewis' momentary deviation from full faith. We saw how we can answer Ellie Wiesel and his objection to the existence of God in a world full of evil. We have discovered that death is not the created order. Death is the direct result of the curse upon this creation as a direct result of the sin of Adam. We also discover that this world's evil has our own signature on it. Every time I sin or you sin, there is an increase in the evil of this world. We contribute to the evil of this world daily. We have further observed that the death curse is linked to the cross. The *Son of the Woman* prophecy in Genesis 3:15 promises that this Son will crush the head of the serpent, Satan, but in the process the serpent will strike His heel. The picture is the battle that occurred at the cross.

Read carefully to what follows:

If you compromise on your interpretation of Genesis and say that God used evolution over millions of years, then you will have to consider the story of Adam and Eve as just a myth. The curse is not the cause of death. Death had to be happening for millions, maybe billions of years before human beings evolved or were created. In that case, you have no answer to C. S. Lewis, Ellie Wiesel, or Kevin Horton as they experienced the horror of this world in their lives. If you change the way you interpret Genesis to match the ideas proposed by the majority of the greatest minds in science today, you have no answer to why your loving God created a world like this one. Read how one such scientist views your compromise:

(Lord, please forgive me for this terrible quote.)

Christianity has fought, still fights, and will fight science to the desperate end over evolution, because evolution destroys utterly and finally the very reason Jesus' earthly life was supposedly made necessary. Destroy Adam and Eve and the original sin, and in the rubble you will find the sorry remains of the son of god. [Evolution] take[s] away the meaning of his death. If Jesus was not the redeemer who died for our sins, and this is what evolution means, then Christianity is nothing! [2]

This man understands theology much more than most Christian theologians. To compromise on evolution and millions of years means that the death curse is a myth. The coming of the Son of the Woman prophecy is myth. He is absolutely right in saying that evolution is a direct affront on the meaning of the entire Bible. This is not a minor issue!

Now think about this:

The Bible, taken literally, implies that the earth is about 6,000–10,000 years old. The flood of Noah was about 4,500 years ago. In contrast, consider again the quote of prominent humanist writer Stephen Jay Gould:

---

[2] G. Richard Bozarth, "The meaning of Evolution," *American Atheist*, February 1978, pp. 19, 30

The human species has inhabited this planet for 250,000 years or so—roughly .0015 percent of life, the last inch of the cosmic mile.

Which view matches reality? Which view matches what we observe? The cradle of civilization is in the region of the Fertile Crescent, the Tigris-Euphrates valley of Iraq and Syria. This is exactly where the Bible says people traveled to after leaving the ark. When we excavate ruins of cities in this land, we discover that there exist ruins that go back about 4,500 years. Below that, there exists no evidence of human existence. Did you get that? Look at that number. We have evidence of human civilization that goes back 4,500 years. There is no evidence of human existence before that. Where is the evidence of the other 245,000 years of human existence that Dr. Gould so forcefully proclaimed? It does not exist. Worldwide, there exists little evidence of human existence much beyond 4,500 years ago!

So who are you going to believe?

If you compromise on how you interpret Genesis, you have no answer to why this world is like it is and you have a 245,000 missing years of human existence!

I go with the Bible.

END NOTES

Chapter 1

[i]   There are many articles that discuss this horrible failure of medicine. A fine article is found in Wikipedia: https://en.wikipedia.org/wiki/Ignaz_Semmelweis

[ii]   In this theory of disease, sickness occurs when the body gets out of balance of the four basic humors. These were described as yellow bile, black bile, phlegm, and blood. We can see that these "humors" are simply some of the fluids that the body produces. This practice was described by Hippocrates in *On the Nature of Man*. He said this: "The human body contains blood, phlegm, yellow, and black Bile. These are the things that make up its constitution and cause its pains and health. Health is primary that state in which these constituent substances are in the correct proportion to each other, both in strength and quantity, and are well mixed. Pain occurs when one of the substances presents either a deficiency or an excess, or is separated in the body and not mixed with the others." *W.N. Mann (1983). G.E.R. Lloyd, ed. Hippocratic writings. Translated by J Chadwick. Harmondsworth: Penguin. p. 262. ISBN 978-0140444513.*

[iii]   Bloodletting involved cutting an artery or vein and draining out a quantity of blood; this was thought to "balance the humors" and would lead to a cure of disease. In reality, it only weakened the patient.

[iv] Kuhn, Thomas S. *The Structure of Scientific Revolutions*. University of Chicago Press, 1962, 2nd edition 1970, Chicago

[v] By *skeletal structure* I mean that science has basic premises that they use to interpret their observations of the world around them. In Dr. Semmelweis' day, the skeletal structure was the idea of balancing the humors. In our day, the skeletal structure is evolution. Observations that scientists make are interpreted by their basic premises.

[vi] See Joel Barker's DVD *The Business of Paradigms* for greater detail on the power of the paradigm over scientists and business people.

[vii] Dr. Wilder-Smith was born Dec 22, 1915 and died Sept 4, 1995

[viii] Mary H Schweitzer et al, Science 307, 1952 (2005) *Soft-Tissue Vessels and Cellular Preservation in Tyrannosaurus rex.*

[x] This is troubling because evolution requires millions of years. The discovery of actual dinosaur soft tissue is data that is shouting at science. It is shouting that the rock layers are not nearly that old. Soft tissue cannot last that long without decay back to basic elements.

[xi] Photos by author at the John Day Fossil Beds National Monument

[xii] Incidentally, this natural breakdown of complex chemicals is exactly opposite of what is predicted to happen in the early evolution of the first cell. Decomposition is what we observe and know to be true. Dead things rot and return to the earth. Chemicals do not spontaneously form complex structures.

[xiii] See the 2011 article from Buckley and Collins that demonstrate under the best conditions collagen will breakdown so that only 1 percent remains after 700,000 years. The article is titled *Collagen survival and its use for species identification in Holocene-lower Pleistocene bone fragments from British archaeological and paleontological sites.* Its website: https://www.research-gate.net/publication/242071735

[xiv] Darwin, Charles, *The Descent of Man and Selection in Relation to Sex.* John Murray, London, 1871.

[xv] Drawing by Melanie Richard

[xvi] Drawing by Melanie Richard—wording by author

[xvii] A great article by Dr. Jerry Bergman titled *Human Embryonic Gills and Gill*

Slits- Down but not out is found at his site: https://creation.com/images/pdfs/tj/j18_1/j18_1_71-75.pdf

Dr. Bergman concludes his article with these words:

> *Unfortunately the gill/gill slit theory remains an icon of evolution and persists in part because it has proven to be a persuasive argument for Darwinism. Although refuted long ago, because skin folds in early vertebrate embryos look superficially similar, many modern authors persist in uncritically citing this idea. Yet it is demonstrably false. Skin folds on the side of the embryonic fish head turn into perforated gill slits with associated gills and respiratory physiology in the adult. Skin folds in the neck region of the human embryo develop into a variety of different organs that have nothing to do with respiration. These facts are widely acknowledged in embryology and anatomy textbooks and scholarly reference sources, but the gill-slit claim is still found in some textbooks and popular sources that discuss Darwinism. Some textbooks do not directly state that humans have gills but rather they misleadingly imply this by their use of terms such as "gill pouches" or "gill furrows." Although most new texts (but not all) now omit this once-common idea, its persistence continues to influence people to accept Darwinism. We urge our readers to write to publishers who persist with this error and graciously ask them to correct it.*

[xviii] See the above endnote for a fine article describing the sequence of events and the invalidity of this theory related to gill slits.

[xix] Photo by author—dock on Flathead Lake, Montana, in early spring. This is similar to the photo by Jodi Cobb (National Geographic Society) that was used to title Dr. Gould's quote in *LIFE Magazine*. I included it to give the quote the same lonely feel.

[xx] Dr. Gould is quoted in *LIFE Magazine*, "The Meaning of Life, The Big Picture," December 1988. By David Friend and the editors of LIFE. The author has the original publication on file. The following is an internet site

that contains this quote: http://www.maryellenmark.com/text/magazines/
life/905W-000-037.html

Chapter 4

^{xxi} All candle photos by author

^{xxii} I would like to acknowledge Mike Riddle and Dr. Bob Compton for excellent work on this subject in their *The Origin of Life Equipping Course*

^{xxiii} For a New Testament example, see the apostle Paul's reference to the "Third Heaven" in 2 Corinthians 12:2.

^{xxiv} Josh McDowell is a Christian apologist (a person who defends the Christian faith). He coined the phrase "to check your brains at the door" in reference to the idea that intellectuals had to ignore reality to believe the Bible. His work proved that just the opposite was true. He spent his life making it clear that Christians have the best intellectual position of anyone. I recommend that everyone read his work *Evidence that Demands a Verdict*. In 2011, Josh McDowell and Bob Hostetler published a book titled, *Don't Check Your Brains at the Door*. Tommy Nelson

^{xxv} Morris, Henry, *The Genesis Record*. Baker Book House, Grand Rapids, 1976, pg. 58. Though Morris notes that the Hebrew word here could mean both outer space or the atmosphere, he concludes, "The firmament referred to in this particular passage is obviously the atmosphere."

^{xxvi} Hebrew [Rakim] Brown-Driver-Briggs Hebrew and English Lexicon defines this as an "extended surface or an expanse (something solid that is being beaten out). This latter idea gives the idea of metal being beaten so that it stretches. Genenius' Hebrew-Chaldee Lexicon of the Old Testament defines it this way, "The firmament of heaven, spread out...."

^{xxvii} See Dr. John Sanford's detailed work, *Genetic Entropy & the Mystery of the Genome*. Dr. Sanford is a geneticist at Cornell University. He was forced to rethink his views on evolution because of his work and extensive knowledge in his field.

^{xxviii} ibid

^{xxiv} ibid

xxx D. Russel Humphreys has an appendix notation listing the 17 verses: Job 8:9, Ps 104:2, Isa 40:20, Jer 10:12, Zec 12:1, 2 Sam 22:10, Job 26:7, Ps 19:9, Ps 144:5, Isa 42:5, Isa 44:24, Isa 45:12, Isa 28:13, Isa 51:13, Jer 51:15, Ezek 1:22. See D. Russel Humphreys, *Starlight and Time*, Master Books, Forest Green, AK, 2000, pg. 66

xxxi Ibid pg. 11–12

xxxii Dawkins, Richard, *The Selfish Gene*. Oxford University Press, New York, 1976, pg. 1

xxxiii According to numerous sources the date of about 3.8 billion years is when life was thought to have spontaneously arisen. For one example, see BBC Nature. Here is a link to the quote below: http://www.bbc.co.uk/nature/history_of_the_earth:

> The history of life on Earth began about 3.8 billion years ago, initially with single-celled prokaryotic cells, such as bacteria. Multicellular life evolved over a billion years later and it's only in the last 570 million years that the kind of life forms we are familiar with began to evolve, starting with arthropods, followed by fish 530 million years ago (Ma), land plants 475Ma and forests 385Ma. Mammals didn't evolve until 200Ma and our own species, Homo sapiens, only 200,000 years ago. So humans have been around for a mere 0.004 percent of the Earth's history.

xxxiv One example of how people believe the DNA code came into existence is found in Richard Dawkins' book, cited above, *The Selfish Gene*. Chapter 2 discusses "The Replicators" in which Dawkins lays out his statement of faith that these early genes just spontaneously arose. He calls this on page 16 as "exceedingly improbable."

xxxv Bacteria are of a class of cells that are called by biologists as prokaryotic. This means that the cellular organelles are not well defined and visible under the microscope. The functions of the cell are the same. They just do not have nearly as well organized sites for those functions. Every one of the functions of the eukaryotic cells organelles (like described in this chapter) still must take place within prokaryotic cells. Apparently, bacteria do not require the high level of organization in their cellular respiration.

xxxvi Quote from Rick Blizzard, D.B.A., Health Editor, Gallup News. Quoted from the following site: http://news.gallup.com/poll/7999/Teens-Acutely-AwareSuicide-Problem.aspx?g_source=link_NEWSV9&g_medium=tile_1&g_campaign-=item_7666&g_content=Teens percent2520Acutely percent2520Aware percent2520of percent2520Suicide percent2520Problem

xxxvii Rachels, James. *Created from Animals, The Moral Implications of Darwinism.* Oxford 1990, pages 80, 82. Downloadable PDF: http://www.jamesrachels.org/CFA.htm

xxxviii https://www.snopes.com/fact-check/iceland-eliminated-syndrome-abortion/

xxxix Scudellari, Megan, *The Sex Paradox*, Cover story, The Scientist, July, 2014 edition Online link: https://www.the-scientist.com/?articles.view/articleNo/40333/title/The-Sex-Paradox/

xl Kelly, Sandra, et.al, "Gender Differences in Brain and Behavior: Hormonal and Neural Bases," *Pharmacology Biochemistry and Behavior.* Vol. 64, No. 4, pp. 655–664, 1999

xli Williams CL, Meck WH. "The organizational effects of gonadal steroids on sexually dimorphic spatial ability." *Psychoneuroendocrinology.* 1991; 16 (1–3):155–76. Review. PubMed PMID: 1961837.

xlii *Meaning of* τεκνογονία. The literal meaning of the noun τεκνογονία is certainly "childbearing." The question is whether it is used literally or figuratively in this passage. A literal view seems improbable here, since not all women bear children.[65] Further, τεκνογονία may refer not only to child-bearing but also to child-rearing.[66] This suggests that a far more probable explanation of the term is that it serves as a synecdoche of the part for the whole. That is, childbearing represents "the general scope of activities in which a Christian woman should be involved." Quoted from: "Women in Ministry: An Exegetical Study of 1 Timothy 2:11–15." Ann L. Bowman *Faculty, Department of Biblical Studies* International School of Theology, San Bernardino, California *Bibliotheca Sacra* 149 (1992): 193–213.

xliii   Weisel, Elie. *Night*. Bantam Books, New York, 1960, Chapter 3; this poem is one of the most famous and oft-quoted statement in this dark and terrible, yet absolutely vital book.

xliv   This quote is from C. S. Lewis as he reflected on Elie Weisel's experiences

xlv   Jb 26:13 *fleeing serpent*, of eclipse-dragon (cf. לִוְיָתָן 3:6); also בְּרַח ... לִוְיָתָן נ' Is 27:1 (symbol. of world powers); נ' of sea-monster [xlv] Francis Brown, Samuel Rolles Driver, and Charles Augustus Briggs, *Enhanced Brown-Driver-Briggs Hebrew and English Lexicon* (Oxford: Clarendon Press, 1977).
        Page . Exported from Logos Bible Software,

xlvi   Ezekiel 28 describes the fall of Satan into sin. Pay attention to verse 15 and later to how pride led up to this terrible event.

xlvii   For a great article on animism, see Dr. Pat Zukeran's work at this site: https:// probe.org/the-world-of-animism/

xlviii The Hebrew word we translate into "serpent" can also be translated into "reptile." The same holds true in Revelation where the Greek word for "dragon" implies that the serpent was originally a reptile like a dinosaur.

xlix   NOTE: Eve (the woman, will be given this name, commonly translated as Eve, at the end of chapter 3: Hebrew is actually "cHava." This name was later translated into a Greek name which sounds like Eve. Eve is a transliteration of the Greek name Ευαν.)

l   When this text was translated into Greek around 200 BC, the Jewish translators viewed the "cool of the day," which means the breezy time of day as the evening. We cannot be certain what time of day this actually means.

li   This prophecy was passed on through many generations until it was formally written by Moses. It is my position that this was more than oral tradition. I believe that there were written works by various authors that Moses compiled to make the book of Genesis (at about B.C. 1400). These different works are marked in the Hebrew by a word (תּוֹלְדוֹת) (*tô·lĕ·ḏōṯ*) that is translated as "generations or account" See Gen 2:4, 5:1, 6:9, 10:1, 11:10, 11:27. These 6 different "Toleldot's" reference the books that Moses complied, under the inspiration of the Holy Spirit, to make Genesis. That would make this prophecy originally written at least 6000 years ago.

lii   For more on the prophecies of the Bible that are literally fulfilled in Jesus, I recommend you consider the works of Josh McDowell. Josh was an avowed atheist who took a year out of his college studies to research Jesus with the goal of debunking Christianity. Eight months into his research, he became a Christian. The evidence was too overwhelming for Jesus being the Messiah. Consider reading his works. A good condensed version is *A Ready Defense: The Best of Josh McDowell*, By Bill Wilson, Thomas Nelson, Nashville. See section two for some of the prophecies of the Old Testament that were fulfilled in Jesus.

liii   Three moms? Three boys from my first wife, Corinne; I have a stepson who came to me in my second marriage to Tatjana; Tatjana and I adopted our only daughter—three moms for five children!

liv   The information about the perpetrators of the Columbine shooting were heard firsthand by the author of this book when Rachel Scott's father, Darrel Scott, came to Missoula, MT. Rachel Scott was the first person killed by Dylan Klebold and Eric Harris.

CPSIA information can be obtained
at www.ICGtesting.com
Printed in the USA
LVHW042149250221
679974LV00002B/2

9 781595 557865